GAIL MORGAN was born [in] 1953. Educated at the Unive[rsity] gained a Master of Arts in En[glish] between writing and her caree[r] foreign language. This work has taken her all over the world and brought her into contact with many different peoples, including the aborigines of the Central Australian desert and the mountain villagers of the Huon Peninsula in Eastern New Guinea. She lived for a number of years in London and France before returning to Sydney where she teaches English to refugees and immigrants from South East Asia, Eastern Europe and Latin America.

The author of poems and plays, *Promise of Rain* is Gail Morgan's first novel. A rich blend of reminiscence and discovery, disillusionment and hope, it takes in the worlds both of suburb and outback in its evocation of the forces which shape the life of a young woman growing up in post-war Australian society.

Promise of Rain
Gail Morgan

Published by VIRAGO PRESS Limited 1985
41 William IV Street, London WC2N 4DB

Copyright © Gail Morgan 1985

All rights reserved

British Library Cataloguing in Publication Data
Morgan, Gail
   Promise of Rain.
   I. Title
   823[F]   PR9619.3.M/
ISBN 0-86068-613-2
ISBN 0-86068-618-3 Pbk

Typeset by Clerkenwell Graphics and
printed in Great Britain by Anchor-Brenden, Tiptree

To my brother
ROBERT SCOTT MORGAN

Why do you come every day to my grave? (He says)
(She says) Your burial posts are painted and ready.
But why do you come each day to this grave?
(She says) Your fine painted posts are unsteady.

(He says) Get up from my grave, wife
I saw you dancing just now.
Dancing and wailing full-life now.
You shake in the dance,
You quake in the dance.
My fine, painted posts are unsteady.

(He says) Why not come to me here,
Why not come where I lie,
Lie beside me here, are you ready?
(She answers) I'm not old,
I'm too young.
And my breasts are like rock.
I can see every flea
that jumps on your dog.

(He says) You know I am here
I'm glad my wife's near.
Near to me now and waiting.

Are you thirsty? (He asks)
Dear one, drink now.
For when I come there'll be none.
I'll show you a dry and waterless country.

*Adapted from mortuary song
sequence, Melville and
Bathurst Islands*

Part 1

1

Lucy Stapleton played carelessly at jacks under the hot glass of an Australian February. Her game, in the heat, was soothing and repetitive, like a trickle of warm water over the dry schoolyard ground.

The other children were playing captive, making their lonely concessions to a convict ancestry. Prestige went to the victim. The Cooper girl, head held close to the ground, was being made to eat dirt and feather.

'Hold her down. Hold her down. Where's her tongue?'

Clouds of whitewash marked the preparation for her blazer rubbing. Lucy looked across, taking for granted the ritual which was as pale and well known to her as the nuns' faces. The walls of the convent fowlhouse would be beaten with a broom until a white mist rose. Then Joylene Cooper would be lamington-rolled against them until her dark blazer was speckled in white.

Lucy had paid with half a show bag for her last turn at being victim. The boys never had to pay, unless they had dandruff. She wondered about the Cooper girl. A whole show bag perhaps?

Sitting under the only gum in the yard, Lucy and her friend Adelaide paused in their game of jacks. They looked upwards, towards the noise of a crow. Play stopped in deference to the black predator which, as Lucy's grandfather had told her, could pluck out the eyes of a new-born lamb as easily as she could make toast for breakfast.

When she swept up the animal knuckles again, clouds of red dust rose.

'I'm up to fours now. You're still on threes.'

'But your hands are bigger than mine,' said Lucy, measuring her own hand carefully against her friend's.

'Did you see what Wayne Thompson got from his father?' asked Adelaide. 'A pack of seventy-two Derwents. That's unbelievable isn't it?'

'In one of those fold-out boxes?' asked Lucy, regretfully.

'Of course. They only come in fold-out boxes,' Adelaide said. 'If he loses the box the pencils will never fit into his pencil case. He can't draw. He can't even colour. I bet he's only going to use them for swapping.'

'He did that drawing once,' said Lucy, 'of Mother de Bosco, so as he'd be made milk monitor.'

'So as he can water the milk,' said Adelaide bitterly. 'So as he can put in little sticks to poison Gerald Smythe. He's never thirsty himself, he just drinks everybody else's out of spite.'

'He's probably thirsty,' said Lucy, 'if he drinks everyone else's. I can tell when mine's been watered because the cap's loose.'

Unaware of their disapproval, of contempt gluing itself to the back of his neck, Wayne was conducting his own favourite game of barter. This usually involved exchange of goods, but occasionally goods for services formed part of the bargain. He had already acquired three comics this month, two sets of bus ticket butts, sherbet with licorice sucking pipes, a gold skull ring with ruby eyes. Meanwhile, he had lost three of his new Derwents, a windmill pencil sharpener and a last year's show bag.

Wayne stopped his trading for a few minutes in order to take stock of the playground. He often did this, especially when his goods were on display, like gold nuggets in the dry unpromising sandstone of Five Dock.

As he gratefully acknowledged the strange exotic brilliance of his possessions, he could not see why, when others linked arms to sing 'Who Wants to Play', he was not included. Recently he had had to pay to be victim. But trading had prepared him well for life's inequalities, or was it vice versa?

As far as Wayne Thompson could see, there was only one hopelessly intractable commodity in his life. It was Lucy Stapleton, whose graceful indifference set his soul alight. There were those who despised him, but none could show such sublime indifference. He looked towards her as she sat under a spindle of gum, her black hair set in a halo of dust, a plaited dusty rope down her back, and two strong quick hands to pick up the jacks.

He wanted to know more about girls, about their soft flaps and entrances, the objects which might go inside. Lucy, he'd heard, played with girls. Private games. They might do all kinds of things together and he would never know. He wanted to draw her, using his Derwents, spread apart without her pants. Pink and tipped with red. He was burning with complicity. Already they seemed to have so much in common. Their mothers played tennis together Saturday mornings.

Suzie and Mavis laughed as they came towards him. 'Down the Mississippi if you miss a loop you're out.' They sang the skipping song. He smiled at them, as that was what everyone else did.

They began to sift through his treasures, burying his skull ring, scratching his monitor's badge, until finally they found an acrobatic monkey which had lost most of its fur. They picked it up, managing to disengage a few of its remaining hairs. No major injury was done. They had ruled in the dusty playground for too long to risk anarchy.

'Does that monkey really do tricks?' asked Suzie sarcastically.

'Yes it does,' said Wayne, 'it flips over.' If only there wasn't two of them, he thought.

'We said "trick", stupid. You can't call a flip a trick. Nobody would call a flip a trick. Nobody but you, a down and out milk monitor. For me and Mavis, a trick is a trick. It's got to be deceitful, like Sister Nagle when she's collecting money for the missions, or the things magicians do at birthday parties. All right. Let's see him flip over.'

The monkey performed its habitual jerky somersault over the bar, exposing its hairless stomach.

'That was pay-thetic,' they said, 'pay-thetic. Haven't you got anything better than that?'

'I've got lots,' he said proudly.

'Your monkey's got a disease,' said Mavis in a moment of inspiration. 'A skin disease. I'm going to tell Mother. It could be extremely dangerous for all of us.'

'It can't have a disease,' said Wayne, his ears distending with fear. 'It's not real. It's made of tin. Dopey old dead tin.'

'With cat's fur,' said Mavis. 'There's still some cat's fur on it. And cats carry disease.'

'My monkey's been sprayed and examined,' he lied.

'Show us its certation then,' said Suzie.

'It's at home,' he said, playing for time. 'The last time I saw it the dog had it.'

'How convenient you are, Wayne Thompson.' Mavis's chin seemed to be guiding her conversation, the prow of a ship, breaking through icebergs. 'Next you'll be telling us the cat certation's been eaten. Let's get out of here Suzie. He's a liar, a liar with a mangy monkey.'

In a few minutes Wayne's treasures were reassembled. He congratulated himself on not having answered back. His property remained intact. The number of times he had warned others, especially Lucy, not to take their bait. But they wouldn't listen. He had seen Lucy playing their game right to the bitter end, until it was too dark to play any further. She would look like a dog scrapping for a bone, miserable and desperate for more. If only he could talk to her one more time, when it was quiet. Perhaps she would see reason at tennis. She would have to learn.

At the end of lunch, the chidren filed into the empty classroom. The wooden smell of rulers, perfume from the Virgin's roses, the honeyed scent of toffee, mixed together. The toffee smell was judged most precious. Toffee was forbidden inside the classroom, and could only be brought in on fingers, hair, uniform. Not even Suzie and Mavis licked toffee under their desks. Everyone knew that Mother de Bosco, like most nuns, had a heightened sense of smell. She could smell illegal toffee, if left unwrapped, from as far away as Ireland.

Lucy, on that humid February day, particularly craved a sticky sticture toffee. As the nun talked she imagined stictures resting in clover. Everything in Ireland rested in clover. Ireland was as green as her grandfather's property in spring, but all year round. It was like a green merry-go-round. If she had been born there she could have become a saint. There weren't any in Australia. Australia was too young. Too young in religion, and too old in geography, as the nuns said.

She was too young. But one day she would be old, like the nuns. And then her nose would bite into smells like a king brown in early spring.

The remembered smells of school holidays span about Lucy like a top. There was the stale meat of cattle dogs, the shiny black droppings of sheep which smelled after rain. Eucalypt, fire, the acid of peppercorns and the yielding smell of imported Monterey pine. All this kept Five Dock out of her nose, the part which dealt with tuckshop mothers, the backs of their ears smelling of dead flowers, or the nuns, who used cheap fatty soaps to keep themselves clean. Her own smells were bad enough, and it was a wonder that Adelaide still wanted to play with her.

Suzie was Mother de Bosco's pet, so she was asked to clean the blackboard. She took a long time to remove the coloured chalk, and on her way back pinched Lucy. Not to be outdone by her friend, Mavis was eye-slitting the Cooper girl, who hadn't yet paid for being victim.

Lucy envied and pitied the Cooper girl. The Cooper girl envied and pitied Lucy. For these reasons the two girls would rarely share a see-saw together after school.

Singing hymns to herself, glazing her eyes over, Lucy waited for the bell to ring. Only the best students were allowed to ring it. They didn't put so much energy into its binary motion. Ireland, she said to herself, where the praties grow. Praties were a more delicate variety of potato and infinitely more edible.

In Ireland nuns had good tempers, because that was their home. It was a de-snaked place. Saint Patrick had cleared them all out so people could swim neck deep in grass. For hundreds of years saints had been able to walk in that country without getting bitten.

The only problem was that a few lessons back they had done Saint Luke. He'd said that saints and people in the Bible had the power to tread on snakes, even scorpions, without getting bitten. That made her wonder why Saint Patrick had bothered clearing them out. She couldn't believe that the saints in Ireland had less treading power than others. But on the other hand, the same treading power would have made Saint Patrick himself redundant. It was yet another mystery. But the advantage of religious mysteries was that they couldn't be solved. The bell rang.

'Are you going to tennis on Saturday?' Wayne asked her.

'Yes,' she answered suspiciously, 'what does that mean?'

'Nothing,' he said, clearing his throat. 'I'll see you there, that's all.'

'Go away,' said Adelaide, moving close to finish him with an impatient push, a dark stretch of face. There wasn't much time before their buses came, and she wanted to talk to Lucy about kidnapping. It was a most interesting and relevant crime to both of them, an unlawful abduction into the adult world, to be wanted by someone with ugly stubble, to be touched, wrapped in a blanket, a jewel, before the murder took place.

They whispered together the distance of Fairlight Street. There were mothers now in place of nuns, wearing headscarves and pulling their shopping behind them on wheels. Only their frowns promised friction. The bus would soon arrive to take Lucy to Haberfield, a suburb where headscarves changed into hats, a place where she had lived all her life.

When the mothers played together the following Saturday, it was on a complex of courts next to a park which in turn was next to a canal, a dingy geometric trickle into the harbour. The air was sticky and wet, thick with blowflies, scratched thin with sandflies. The mothers arranged themselves uncomfortably on their sandy battleground. Lucy watched her mother, playing carefully as if at a tennis lesson.

Next to the courts a steely playground glistened with anticipated life. In front was the car park, a row of Holdens behind a broken fence. The overall effect was one of brilliance forged without compromise by chrome in the sun.

Lucy ran to her favourite swing, fashioned out of steel. It had the skeletal shape of a ship, salvaged, she imagined, from the canal at the time it had lost its water. She swung backwards and forwards in pendulum motion, soothing for a young girl on a hot day. As yet the swing hadn't grown too uncomfortable in the heat. So she lay on its base, facing the sky.

In the distance she could hear the anxious, apologetic shrieks of her mother's friends. She tried to time her even rocking to the noise of the tennis ball back and forth. It would be a lovely new white tennis ball. White and as fluffy as a new-born lamb. She imagined a series of lambs in single file, waiting to be made into tennis balls, to see their fleeces bounce happily away.

While the other children were arriving she sang very softly: 'Baa baa black sheep. Have you any wool? Yes sir, yes sir, a tennis racquet full.'

'Come and play on the roundabout, Lucy,' a voice shouted. It wanted her swing.

'No thanks,' she said, looking over the greasy head. 'I'm happy where I am.'

Everything was clear from a position of invulnerability. Backwards up, forwards up. Her feet seemed to be paddling in the sky and drying themselves on their downward flight. A perfect inter-dependence. If only she could get someone to push her, then she would go really high. She needed someone to push her, a vassal – like Wayne Thompson, who had just arrived. A look and smile would bring him over, a small price to pay for his assistance.

'Someone told me your Dad bought you a box of seventy-two Derwents,' said Lucy politely, trying to ignore his bony arms which had begun to push her jerkingly into the sky. 'Adelaide told me.' She tucked her dress carefully under her. He seemed to be looking there.

'Yes,' he said impatiently. There were more important issues to be discussed, now she had time to listen. He gave the swing a determined push. If only he could touch her as she came down, the subsequent thrust upward would absolve him from responsibility. Lying down, legs splayed like plaits, on the base of the swing, she was irresistible. Her eyes, an intense blue, reflected the sky. He wanted to push her soft mouth into the metal of the swing before kissing her, to make her aware of the contrast.

'I think,' he said seriously, 'that the two of us should ignore Suzie and Mavis and become boyfriend and girlfriend. Lucy, will you be?'

'What?'

'My girlfriend. Most people have a girlfriend. One. You can be mine.'

'But I don't want a boyfriend,' said Lucy, not wanting to feel the desire that was rising inside her. 'And I can't. Adelaide doesn't like you because you sweat so much.'

The sweat, working its way over his body, mocked his exertions. 'Then can I see under your dress again? I can't touch you through the swing, so let me have a look, just one look.'

'Get lost,' she said angrily. 'You belong in a toilet.'

'You belong in a toilet,' he said, thinking regretfully of the cubby hole the nuns had blocked off, 'where I can look at you.'

'Then I'm telling Mother de Bosco on you,' she said. 'You're one of the boys who's been spying on the girls' toilet. You'll get expelled.'

Temporarily Mother de Bosco had become her ally. In matters of chastity she could be trusted absolutely.

'You're not perfect,' he replied bitterly. 'You've got more ideas than I have. I know who you play with. You play with other girls.'

'That's different. Very different.'

'How different then?'

'You know how stealing from your parents is less serious than stealing from a shop?'

'Yes,' he agreed. Mother had told them that.

'Well I play with girls because they're the same sex. And being the same sex is almost the same blood, like parents. If I let you play with me it would be far more serious. It would be a mortal sin, and I'd get it for both of us.'

'I'd get it too,' he said. 'I'd get the sin too. And the same sex is not the same blood neither.'

'Yes it is.'

'No it's not. You're blind,' he said, 'like my rosella. Whenever I put the cover on its cage, she thinks it's night.'

'Then she must want it to be night,' said Lucy, 'so she

doesn't have to look at your feed tray, or your cuttlefish bone, or think about the insects she can never eat, or look at your sweating hand replacing her tray of water when she's not thirsty.'

'Who said I had a cuttlefish bone?' Wayne asked with considerable aggression. He hadn't told her about it before.

'Nobody,' she said. 'But you make me think of a blind ram. It'll run in a circle until it dies.'

'We're talking about my rosella, aren't we?'

'And what if your bird got out of its cage, it'd only find itself here.' Lucy looked sorrowfully across the canal separating Haberfield from Five Dock. It held a thick bog of mud which attracted animals. Once down, the poor creatures could not climb back up the slippery sides of the channel.

'What's wrong with here? What's wrong with Five Dock?'

'I don't like it,' said Lucy, 'and my mother prefers the country, and my father would like to live on the South Coast.'

'I'm going to live in Five Dock for the rest of my life,' said Wayne, making Lucy ashamed of her disloyalty. 'I know it stinks at low tide, but my mother uses air fresheners, and they've got a lovely smell. She says that you just have to shut the windows at certain times of the day, and that if the smell went she would miss it greatly. I know Haberfield is better.'

'I didn't say it was,' said Lucy, very much surprised.

'It's better because there aren't any hotels, and the houses are bigger. There are better types in Haberfield, that's what Mum says. Then where will you live if you don't like Haberfield and you don't like Five Dock?'

'Ireland,' she said, factually, losing patience with the boy, the yellow grains of sleep crushed into the rims of his eyes. 'Dublin. And it's in Dublin that I'll spend my dubloons.' She exaggerated the final crooning syllable in the manner of a parish priest.

'If you're trying to be a brain,' he said, 'then you're dumb.'

'You'll never understand,' she said regretfully. The nuns didn't either. If only their eyes would, one day, shine some soft approval on her. She needed their acceptance so she could tell her own future. But their eyes were always too full of doom to be looked at.

'You'll never understand,' she repeated methodically.

'Yes I will,' he said, jumping onto the back of the swing. 'And I'm going to take you to Ireland.'

He bent his knees in a furious pushing motion, until the swing was high in the sky. The precarious aggression brought an audience from all corners of the park.

'We know your girlfriend,' they sang. 'Push her higher. She'll hold on. She'll have to.'

'But I can't,' cried Lucy. 'It's too slippery on the bottom. I think the chains are going to break.'

'Hold on to me,' said Wayne, laughing rudely.

The spectators were delighted as Lucy slid dangerously on the base of the swing. Some of them were envious.

By the time the swing had stopped, the sky was still moving for Lucy. She tried to stand up, but dizziness forced her down, like a ewe which too long in labour on one side, loses its balance and is unable to return to the herd.

'Your ears have got red,' he said, amused at the changes he'd wrought in her appearance.

'And your ears are uglier than Michael Fish's.' She spat on the ground, wanting to kick him, but fearing retaliation which would have been more humiliating. One day, when he wasn't ready, she'd punch him hard on the ear flaps so he'd lose his balance.

'Of course you know,' she said, 'that your ugly ears have been stretched by the devil. And one day,' she paused, trying to think of something to say, 'he'll take them back, when he comes to take your soul. You'll be deaf, and blind from looking in girls' toilets, and nobody'll recognise you, especially me.'

'Do you want some of my sherbet?' he asked, taking some reconciliation out of his pocket.

'Give it to Michael Fish,' she said, disappointed that her contempt was so ineffectual. If only she could punch him hard and knock his brains out on the concrete. But whatever she did, he'd turn it into a wrestle, and he would enjoy wrestling with girls.

Lucy ran to the car park to seek refuge in her parents' Holden. When her tears came, they were hot midday tears that burned her face as they dried. Cicadas, with their loud masking magic, invited her to sleep, to sing about girlfriends until they no longer counted. The smell of car plastic was reassuring; she felt protected, her mother was playing tennis, and all was still except for the safe sluggish movement of flies.

'Girlfriend. Girlfriend. We know.'

Lucy slept her sleeping escape. Meanwhile, with the righteousness of the uninvited, a crowd began to gather round the car.

'Kiss 'er Wayne, kiss 'er, she's asleep.'

As their voices were getting louder and more determined, Lucy woke.

'Can't you see I'm trying to sleep,' she said angrily, locking all the doors except one, which Wayne had just as quickly opened and locked behind him. Perhaps for the first time in his life he found himself at a loss.

Squashed faces were telling him to kiss her. He repeated what he thought they were saying. 'Go on,' he said, 'kiss her all over.'

Alarmed, he fumbled with Lucy as if she were something hot from the oven. He kissed her furiously and anxiously.

'You're my girlfriend,' he said. 'Now you're my girlfriend.'

He pinched where there were no breasts and tried to feel underneath her dress.

'Stop,' said Lucy. 'That's my mother coming.' She was ashamed rather than relieved, having felt a certain small desire for the boy.

'Sit up straight. Go on, sit up. She'll see us.'

Lucy's mother discerned no guilt in her search for the thermos flask. Nevertheless the two lovers held their breath in fear. They sat erect, and stiff as two wicker car seat covers, until the danger had passed.

Exhausted, Wayne jumped out of the car, unscrewing its petrol cap as a sign of discontent and failure. Lucy, wanting to be rid of the vehicle, ran to the furthest part of the car park, and stood there until tennis was over.

That night at dinner, a new juicy slice of her privacy was carved off.

'By cripes I'm going to find my petrol cap,' said her father. 'I'm not driving around with no dangerous oil rag plugged into me tank, am I Lucy? You're being spoken to. Where is it? You're not too old to get the strap, not too old by a long chalk.'

It wasn't often that her father shed the distracted looks of a gambler. For once, his eyes were keenly focused on her, and this effort of concentration had caused him to over-salt his beef.

'Wayne Thompson,' she said, laying blame on this relatively unknown commodity. 'Wayne Thompson was playing with it. I saw him.'

'Then I'll rat him out,' said her father. 'He lives in Five Dock, Jill. You play tennis with his mother.'

The way her father extracted the truth was like her grandfather pulling out a lamb with a loop of string, dead and midway from its mother.

'It was Wayne Thompson,' she repeated hopelessly,

13

'Wayne Thompson,' knowing that on the next day she would be conscripted back into the car to confront the recreant at his Five Dock bungalow.

The next day the two fathers shook hands at the doorstep. Lucy interpreted this as a highly warlike gesture, and Wayne, not wanting to look at her, cast his eyes upwards to the dull green house-guttering that seemed to be holding up the sky.

As they walked to the car her father insisted they all share the front seat, to facilitate discovery. Wayne pushed his damp legs hard into the car door to avoid contact, and Lucy wondered if the pool of wetness he left on the plastic would be bigger than hers when they got out.

'What way did you and your mother come home?' her father asked, so angry he could barely speak.

'Past where the bus terminates,' Lucy said as they drove along the edge of the water. The tide was out. She could smell flowers long dead in a vase, flowers whose stems had been cut too short, plucked too soon by an eager child, and left to sink back into the tidal flats.

'There it is,' Wayne shouted. 'It's over there, in the gutter.'

The cap was shining like silver amongst the dead leaves.

'Go and get it Lucy,' they said together, Wayne having to let her out of the car in order to do it.

As she picked it up, she pulled an ugly face. The two of them were sitting in co-operative superiority. Same sex, same blood, she thought to herself, a pair of toby jugs, in different sizes, balanced on the car seat.

2

It was late into brisk autumn weather. Lucy was listening to her teacher speak. The nun was blowing breath onto roses, brought by the Cooper girl, as she tantalised the children with descriptions of sin and the paralysing punishment which would follow. The soft petals of the roses moved uneasily as the nun uttered the plosives, 'spiritual' and 'preparation'. Her face was transparent with age, and like air compared to her thick black body which was belted at the waist.

The class looked forward to the day when it would pack along the communion rails, silent and spiritual in organza. Lucy, in spite of the twenty-four-hour fast, was the most enthusiastic of all. She had read books on the subject of transubstantiation and the famous generals who, after their greatest victories, declared the day they made their First Holy Communion as the most important.

The class had learnt a new series of Latin hymns for the occasion. Parents had been harangued to provide suitable raiment. For their children's bodies were to be chalices, and like chalices, had to be heavy, and precious, and encrusted with jewels. The more encrusted they were, the more precious they became to God, and some parents knew that. Lucy expected that her encrustation would not be spectacular, somewhere short of safe middle ground.

Everyone knew that Teresa Simmons was going to look the best. Her mother put her hair in sausage curls just to go to school. Her dress would be multi-layered, and covered in muslin butterflies with small pearls for their eyes. She would take up two places, and everyone else would have to squash in around her.

After the communion mass there was going to be a communion breakfast. Some of the children contrasted in their minds the tender melting of Christ's body without the use of one sacrilegious tooth to this feast which was to follow. By all accounts it would be lavish. There would be a skirmish for the cakes with jam and cream, and the tomato sauce dish, always too small, would be brimful with the dead flakes of sausage rolls.

Lucy looked down with a certain hopeless satisfaction at her saint book. Its edges were crimped by pinking shears, and under each saint was a coloured column. Every time she was good in singing class she coloured the column under Saint Cecilia. She was hoping to find a blind person so she could colour under Saint Lucy, patron saint of the blind. Saint Jude 'hope of the hopeless' bore the brunt of many deeds: when she helped her mother with the garden and stopped when she'd picked up a caterpillar, when she'd polished the class statue of Our Lady and the gilt had rubbed off, and when she'd sent loose money instead of a postal order to the Spastic Centre and the money never arrived. She had to divide things into categories in order to make a spiritual profit. Her grandfather was always dividing, that was his main occupation: rams from ewes, castrated males from ewes, and lambs from ewes. He had sound reasons for each division.

Nevertheless it was one long struggle, and only the nuns were safe. Their habits protected them, like camouflage, ready for when He comes like a thief in the night.

Mother de Bosco adjusted the white coif which was pinching her skin. In spite of her pale complexion, she had the look of a peasant, wrinkles drawn like ledger lines around her bright eyes. Lost forever was the look of virgin sacrifice, a look which had abandoned her almost as quickly as a lover might have, an Irish lover.

Why had she been sent to this country? What things had to be done in His name? She found only a chalice of dry dust, every second tree a crucifix stripped of its leaves and as bare as a skull. She could no longer hope that she, a shepherdess with sunstroke, feet swollen and sore, lightning rod for a crook, would ever rejoin her flock.

How naive the local people were. She regarded them with scorn. With newcomers like herself they behaved as the aborigines had first behaved, striving for European acceptance.

'You will soon be making your First Holy Communion,' she began, setting a look upon each member of her class and seeming to jump inside each one of their souls. 'And some of you, I know, come from homes where the family rosary is not said. But do not be afraid. That is why you're making your First Holy Communion; to bring the straying members of your families to God.

'I remember a sad case.' Mother de Bosco's sad cases usually came from Ireland. 'A sad case indeed, where a girl's parents were not good Catholics. When it came time for their daughter to make her communion, they refused point blank to buy her a pair of black patent leather shoes.'

Parental misdemeanour was almost as fascinating to the children as kidnapping. They sat upright with their arms folded neatly in front. ' "Too expensive," the parents said. "Once, twice, three times too expensive." '

The children who hadn't already purchased their footwear were thrown into a panic. Mother de Bosco watched her class gratefully. If there was one vice she detested above immodesty, it was spiritual complacency, a sin accentuated in a people in exile.

'But,' she began again, 'the young girl was not going to

put aside her faith, or diminish the greatness of that great day. She began immediately to save for a pair of appropriate shoes.

'For six months that child went without sweets, not including Lent of course, to save the money. She did little jobs around the house. She debased herself in every way acceptable, until, two days before the Sunday, she found she'd saved enough money to take herself down to the local bootmaker to buy the shoes.

'And when the young girl finally arrived home, she put the glistening black pair into her wardrobe. She put them next to her only other shoes, which were two dirty disgusting rubber thongs.'

Certain members of the class felt uneasy. Thongs were a recent introduction into Five Dock society, but much approved of. Only those veterans of the Great Depression, when shoes had been an important status symbol, would have sympathised with the teacher. But Mother de Bosco abhorred the V-shaped nudity of these new cheap sandals, the way they trussed the toes as if preparing them for the table. She felt no compunction therefore about introducing them as a moral anachronism into her story.

'Unfortunately,' said the nun, clearing her throat conscientiously, before delivering the bad news, 'when the time came for the young girl to dress on that great Sunday morning, she had to face her first real trial as a devout Catholic. Her wicked father had hidden her new shoes!'

The class was shocked. Lucy couldn't imagine a father as wicked as that. Hers was so good by comparison. Even Mavis's father wouldn't have done such a thing, and he was known to have pissed on the side of cars.

The nun continued. Her eyes, crystals, sinking into a vortex of loose skin.

'But,' she said firmly, 'the young girl was undeterred.

She was on fire with the prospect of receiving Christ into her heart. For on that very morning, when the other children were in their best clothes, she proceeded to mass wearing no shoes at all. Thus she was able to prove the strength of her faith to parents and classmates alike.'

'What about her thongs?' the class questioned to themselves. 'What about the thongs in her cupboard? Why did she go barefoot?' Mother de Bosco's stories often lacked neatness. They had a pinching quality, making it difficult to squeeze into the truth.

'Yet,' she said, with the regret of a shopper who'd lost a bargain, 'even with the strongest faiths, and the best intentions, there are pitfalls upon which are too numerous to elaborate.' As the story reached its climax, her grammar became excruciating, meticulous.

'For some months later that same girl, without shoes, was tempted, as we all are from time to time, by the Devil. He spoke to her in a dream, a good place for temptations, telling her if she didn't go to mass then she would get her shoes back from her father. This would enable her to dance in front of boys, which she could only do if she had shoes, exciting their interest and attention.'

The image of the young girl, dancing in white, with her two glittering black feet dipped in chaos, excited the class in the manner of a falling star.

Their teacher waited until she felt it time to say, 'She succumbed. The Devil was able to claim yet another victim. She decided not to go to mass for the first time in her young life, to reclaim the shoes that had never been worn.

'That poor child, as we are all God's poor children, little could she have known God's plan for her. Little could she have known when she went out to play in the park, ice cream in hand, feet shining in black, God's plan.

'Of course she would have been happy for a while, playing on the swings, playing with Protestant boys, when all the decent ones were at Sunday Mass. She would have been very happy for a while, at least until the weather changed, and the sky began to darken, and heavy rain clouds drew a veil of despair over the horizon.'

Teresa Simmons looked at Mother de Bosco's veil and found she could detect despair in its heavy blackness. Most members of the class were sitting forward from their desks, frozen into patterns of hailstones as their teacher spoke.

'The young girl began to have doubts. She asked herself whether or not she would get a second chance. She looked up at the town clock, but realised she'd missed the last mass of the day, the mass for people who have second thoughts. The young girl ran quickly to avoid her destiny. But the rain fell heavy upon her. It fell down in heavy beads, like my wooden rosary.'

A hand raised.

'No Jane. It wasn't a miracle; just one way that nature reflects God when He is angry.

'I shouldn't have to tell you how the poor child was struck down. Left, when the lightning had finished with her, a burnt stump, face forward in a bed of lilies.

'God only knows if she was forgiven.' The nun took one long final pause. 'But on the basis of church law, we can assume she was damned to the fires of hell.'

Several members of the class took the opportunity to assert their faiths. Some, in nervous reflex, made signs of the cross. But still a question remained unanswered: what was wrong with thongs? Hadn't they been vindicated in the story? For if the young girl had been wearing rubber footwear, she wouldn't have been killed by the lightning.

Nevertheless many acts of contrition were made. The heat in the classroom rose slowly, carrying its burden of prayer, and no fresh air seemed willing to come in to replace it. The Cooper girl asked permission to open a window, but it was refused.

Lucy was worried. Her teacher had implied two things. The first was that wickedness could be inherited; the young girl had had such a wicked father. The second was that He waited for a mortal sin to be committed before He played His trump card. Who would be safe under these circumstances? Why had God struck the young girl down in the park? Perhaps it was a message to her, and Wayne Thompson.

When it was time for the class to separate, the boys went outside to play rounders and the girls stayed inside to sew. Lucy was making an apron. It was gingham-checked, worked in cross-stitch, and its pattern consisted of three rows of stars. It was a model of blurred geometricity, and caused her teacher considerable amusement. But Lucy couldn't see the use of working to make something to work in, and every time she looked outside at the game of rounders she jabbed her needle into the side of her desk.

Spending a considerable time looking at the apron, without doing anything, Lucy was puzzled with herself for having created such a slur of cross check and star. Her teacher attributed it to what she called 'spiritual Parkinson's disease', which was a degenerative disease of the spirit that blurred the truth.

Lucy looked down sadly at her ambiguous apron. She remembered a time of confusion in the country when her parents had been fighting. She'd run into the thistle paddock to sleep. She'd pretended to be a starfish landlocked on mossy rock, praying to be taken up into the sky and re-made into a star. The shape left behind would have been burnt black, with five sharp thistled points, mourned over by parents and friends.

Their respect would form from and grow out of ignorance.

She felt she was about to cry, but it was time to go

home. Her classmates were beginning to scatter; like a series of crumbs being thrown to pigeons, they waited to be scooped up into parental claws and enjoyed.

Lucy as usual went home by bus. Oftentimes she used her fare money on lollies. Thus she spent many of her trips to Haberfield avoiding, persuading, or lying to the conductor about what had happened to her fare. Occasionally an inspector got on the bus, in which case she would get off immediately; it had been made known to her that she was on the Offenders' List, and could be taken to court upon the next violation.

When she arrived home, her mother was in the kitchen. It was a large room with a disproportionately small cooker, spelt Kooka, the appropriate bird decorating the oven door. It made her mother look like a giant as she transferred the contents of a cream and green canister into a cream and green saucepan, hovering ominously over her cooking.

Lucy compared her mother's awkwardness now, to the times she used Grandfather's wood stove. It had also been the heating system for their bath water, and had to be continually refuelled and stoked. Her mother had reminded her then of a friendly steam-engine driver, whereas now she made a horrible crouching shape over pale jets of gas.

Nothing had been done to the kitchen since the outbreak of war, except for the installation of appliances such as the stove, a toaster, a hand-held cake mixer (electric) and a milk-shake maker. The old linoleum was patterned with black cracks, and one day Lucy had attempted to match their pattern to those made by her mother's veins. But there was little to be gained from such occupations, nor from the kitchen itself. It was a dirt trap, with its creviced floor, its greasy walls and wall tiles edged in black. Lucy and the other members of her family found themselves attracted there, as small insects will fly to what is greasy or sticky, and remain.

'Mum,' said Lucy, sitting at the large wooden table and playing with the bread bin, 'did your hands shake when you were at school? I can't sew because my hands shake.'

'No,' her mother replied. 'How's your apron coming along?'

'It looks strange,' said Lucy. 'The pattern is wrong.'

'But I told you just to do a simple row of flowers. Why can't you do anything I say. You're going to make life very difficult for yourself, and I suppose the other children have nice patterns. I saw Mrs Cooper yesterday. I don't know why you're not more friendly with the Cooper girl. Her daughter's done a little elephant holding a bunch of daisies in its trunk. I wish she had stayed to talk. I'll be starting back at work soon, and I'd like to get to know the mothers before it's too late. But I suppose I made the first mistake by not volunteering for the tuckshop.'

'I hate sewing,' said Lucy. 'I hate it with my heart and my mind and my soul.'

'That's a pity,' said her mother, 'a great pity. When I was your age I was doing tapestry, and chain stitch, and or course stem. I embroidered my first ball gown to wear to the Troccadero.'

'To meet Dad in?' said Lucy.

'I met others before him,' said her mother. 'One of them has done very well in banking since. I'm not surprised. He used to be so well groomed and punctual. He brought my orchid in the most beautifully ironed handkerchief, done up like a knapsack and tied in four corners. Then he would untie each corner and watch my face. But he always brought orchids.'

'Didn't you want orchids?' asked Lucy curiously.

'Yes, but every now and then I wanted something different, like perfume or a single rose, or even a dead lizard.' She laughed.

'Or even a racing ticket,' said Lucy eagerly.

'Yes,' said her mother, sounding disappointed, 'even that.'

'What if he'd brought you an exploding orchid, like those exploding cigars?' Lucy wanted to keep her mother laughing. Laughing made her pretty, like lipstick and soft light. 'And it went off while you were dancing, and your pants fell down.'

'Don't be silly,' said her mother. 'That's not in the least bit funny.'

'Mother de Bosco says I can't write. But it gets worse when she looks over my shoulder.'

'I can't understand that. You read so much. You must keep changing your nib you know, otherwise your writing will look spidery, and whatever you do don't spare the blotting paper. Use the corners to soak up the ink first, and then dry your writing with the rest.'

'It's just that one dip into the inkwell only does two letters, and then they go scratchy, and I have to dip in again and make a blotch because I've got too much ink on my pen.'

'It's practice that's all. Just go light on the upstrokes and heavy on the down, then you'll have beautiful writing. Have you got any good news from school?'

'No. Except that Mother told us a story about a girl who had her shoes stolen, and missed mass, then got struck by lightning.'

'Oh well,' said her mother with resignation, 'you'll be making your First Holy Communion soon.'

'Does Grandfather go to mass every Sunday?' Lucy asked, wondering how far back she would have to go to establish inheritable wickedness.

'He lives in the country,' her mother said gently. 'It's a long way to mass.'

'Mother de Bosco told us that the regulation distance for not going is thirty miles, and he only lives twenty-five miles away, which means his Sunday obligation is still upon him. That's such bad luck isn't it? He should've had his house built thirty miles away from the chapel, and then he wouldn't have to go.'

'There's a lesser obligation on him,' her mother said.

'Then he never really misses mass?' said Lucy, still unsure.

'No. Not really. I bet the poor fellow is sliding around on that clay road right now, fixing the powerlines brought down in the rain that the Shire should be fixing. They've had a lot of rain up there you know. You'll notice a difference in September. It'll be a good lambing.'

There was splendour in a good lambing, exciting in Lucy's mind, a sense of absolution, with each lamb an Agnus Dei, sung or pushed out of its mother, to have its naughty tail circumcised. Grandfather was, and would be forgiven, and she would follow him like a cattle dog, and together they could miss mass every third Sunday.

'When will dinner be ready?' she asked.

'Soon.'

'What are we having?'

'Lamb,' said her mother. 'What's so funny this time?'

'Lamb.'

'Exploding lambs, I suppose,' said her mother.

'Do you know,' said Lucy, 'if a sheep catches fire it has to be wrapped in a woollen blanket immediately – a woollen blanket. It's so funny to think about.'

'Nonsense,' said her mother. She paused, looking rather odd and thoughtful over the stove. 'But I am looking forward to getting out of Sydney. Since the war people seem to have become stall-fed, tasteless meat. There's nothing worse. And nobody will talk.'

'I'll talk,' said Lucy. 'I'm talking.'

'Yes,' said her mother sadly. 'But why don't you like the Cooper girl?'

Later that night Lucy roasted on the spit of her nightmares, turning to meet each infernal variation of pain with mechanical ease. Lambs turned into wolves in her dreams, their coats singed brown and dark, their dry thirsty voices cracking like whips over the graves of the unrepentant.

The moon had become a fortune teller's crystal pawned by its owner. The poor man in a scatter of rags had read his fortune and fled, leaving its cheap secrets to be redeemed.

She dreamed of her silkworms, dangerous pets; they were spinning a moon shroud. A green and disgruntled colour, they awaited their first cause, a mutation from the sky to save them from servitude. It came. It descended and told them to spin themselves together to make a bigger worm, a better worm to devour their sleeping mistress.

In her next dream Lucy was split by lightning. She was de Bosco's young girl. The charcoal stump. Her soul had decided to leave her. Then she had to beg to be back and pushed by the peristalsis of worm lining.

'Come back,' she called to her soul. 'God will give you another chance to look at hell's ever-dying embers. Come back. I know I'm charcoal, like everything down there, but it's what I once was that's important.'

Tears. In the morning her eyes were ringed with water, and her school uniform seemed like her soul, hanging returned on the wardrobe door.

She put on her uniform gratefully, shuddering. Looking in the mirror for change. She could see nothing, no strands of silk flapping from her ears, no charcoal, except for the eyebrow pencil she'd borrowed from her mother. So now she could walk to school free from care, like the roses in the Cooper girl's garden. That poor girl lived across the road from the school, and got into more trouble if she was late. Her neat red-brick house might have been highly desirable if it hadn't faced the convent. Lucy wasn't sure if she was jealous. Certainly her own house was faded, rather dirty.

Lucy passed the main entrance to the school, which was an elaborately worked iron gate with Latin inscription attached to a more economical wooden fence, kept in constant repair by the fathers of the more favoured pupils.

She didn't use the main entrance as no pupil was allowed, unless accompanied by a parent, or in a car. The main drive was pebbled, and became circular around a statue of the Virgin.

The chapel took precedence. Heavy and ornate, it accepted delivery of many goods left by bewildered tradesmen who mistook it for the convent in their embarrassed haste.

The main convent building was Victorian; its architecture binary. It possessed a decorative lace balcony, as well as a more heavy-duty brick verandah, the latter partly closed in. The decorative balcony balanced on the convent's roof like the fading, or rather, the yellowing coif of an indecisive postulant; the verandah was where the older nuns died.

And within the convent there was binary movement. Mother de Bosco and Sister Nagle had fought one another during the many years of their mutual residence. Recently the fighting had become bitter, as the two nuns placed their hope in the more capricious favours of a master who had been absent too long to be remembered, and whose laws had become unseasonable.

Sister Nagle had taken to taunting the other nun with her eccentricities; making a ceremony out of pigeon shooting, allowing her dead birds to be eaten by the convent's, or rather, Mother de Bosco's cat, who left behind the merest scratching of blood and beak.

In reply, Mother de Bosco had had a fowlhouse

installed under Sister Nagle's bedroom window, and had received a commendation from the archdiocese authorities for her dedication and persistence in the matter.

For Mother de Bosco had a delicate stomach, and indeed the only full-length mirror in the convent with which to view it. She imagined the other nun, the dribble and gurgle of her prayers, her senile evocation of a heavenly coronation, where she would form a maypole for all the little cherubs to dance around and caress. She was the only nun in the convent still menstruating. It was disgusting.

One of the reasons for this state of civil war was undoubtedly the strange arid country in which they lived, where even the Protestants were refusing to persecute them. There were certain political issues of course, which kept the two religions apart, but the real hatred was gone, and while the Catholics worshipped their statues, the Protestants had other, more profitable false gods to worship. It was in fact a mixed marriage, where little attention would be given to the religion of the offspring.

Mother de Bosco felt she'd been abandoned in her new country. Her links with her homeland were rusting. The superior social station she'd held in Ireland had vanished, and she felt no better than a policewoman consecrated to serve God. Thus, ironically enough, she confirmed the well-established trend for the Irish to enter the constabulary in the first generation.

She envied those Spaniards of a few centuries before. They had had a country to return to, as those who conquer do. They would have been able to boast of daring deeds and obtain absolution. Here she felt there was no turning back.

'Just before religion class,' she began, irritably, in spite of the relatively cool weather, 'and now that we've finished prayers, I'd like to correct last night's homework.'

There was an ominous hushed reaction to her announcement. The nuns were at their most irascible after prayers. Homework was usually corrected in the afternoon, to give the children an opportunity to copy or complete it over lunch. Thus few had done the required work.

'All right,' she said, playing with her chin and picking out the most pathetically Irish member of her class, the parody of Gaelic elfishness, which the nuns for the sake of sanity had rejected. 'Lucy Stapleton. You fancy yourself a geographer, exploring the hedge that Mr Ryan has expressly forbidden the children of this school to explore.'

Disappointed, she stood up. The rest of the class was tense. If Lucy hadn't done her homework, someone else would be asked, then someone else, until the most exact statistics were gained.

'Well dear, what is a cape?' The nun paused. 'And I hope you've done the illustration.'

'A cape,' said Lucy, 'is the material a bull-fighter drapes over his arm. It operates as bait for the bull, who is bred for his fighting prowess, in Spain.'

Lucy held up her drawing of a golden matador, with his red cape, jewel-spangled, a glittering whirlpool which seemed to be inviting the half-drawn beast to come forward onto the page and complete itself.

'You fool,' said her teacher, surprised by the naivety of her least favoured pupil. 'It's not possible. You're nearly nine years old. Too old for this class. Who else put your answer?'

No one volunteered. Some were curious as to when it would be safe to laugh.

'A cape,' said the nun, 'is a piece of land jutting out into the water.'

'I'm sorry,' said Lucy. 'I didn't realise. I looked it up in the dictionary, then added a little bit myself.'

'The road to hell, my dear, is paved with good intentions, and dictionaries are one of their many repositories. Words can be twisted to suit ourselves. The word "cape" has two meanings, so you choose the one that would suit you, rather than myself. It's quite simple. You thought you could do your homework and suit yourself at the same time. How we can delude ourselves. But actions will always speak louder. In fact, if you weren't too old for this class I would recommend to your parents that you repeat. But time waits for no man, especially for someone like you, who walks, talks, and thinks so slowly. I've often wondered whether there's a lead weight in your skull. Is there? Is there a lead weight there?'

'I don't know what's in my head,' said Lucy sobbing.

'Come on. You're too big to be crying like this. God will forgive you,' said Mother de Bosco in her most matter-of-fact tone. 'God forgives the slowest of His creatures. He made the humble snail, didn't He? Haven't you brought a handkerchief to school?'

'If she borrows my handkerchief,' whispered Mavis, 'she'll leave a trail of silver snot in it.'

'Silver snot,' whispered Suzie, laughing. 'Silver snot, silver snot, silver snot.'

Suzie and Mavis coalesced in the sublime moment of Lucy's failure, like two raindrops meeting in some base estuary. She knew her failure would be reinforced after school. Friends had good memories.

It was hard for Lucy to understand these two. As individuals they were capable of the highest flights of macabre imagination. Mavis on a swing was a graceful princess, watching full of love over her subjects below. Suzie's kingdom, by virtue of exclusion, was an earthly one. Between them they divided up the world.

However, once together, no easy transformation took place. Disliking the tuning fork, they would adopt the adder's tongue. Lucy could accept it, only because some of the time they were kind to her.

3

Of all the nuns who daily wept thunder from the skies, Sister Nagle, choirmistress, was the most humble. Her main joy in the earthly time allotted her, apart from the occasional malicious triumph over Mother de Bosco, was to paint flowers with lead-based house paint.

Many painstaking hours were spent as this noble savage served her concept of beauty. Painted geraniums grew in abundance around the bubblers. There were black-spotted roses in the remoter parts of the playground. The animate, the kinetic, made meaningful through woman. God be praised, she said to herself.

It was Sister Nagle's job to take Lucy's class for singing, and to prepare them for their end-of-year concert. 'Holy. Holy. Holy. Lord God of power and might. Heaven and earth are filled with your glory' at the mere raising of her hand. One day, as she used to say with a modest laugh, her choir would be a perfect one, and instead of chatter, there would only be the rustling of heavenly wings, silken and quiet.

The group assembled for that day. Adelaide talked to the Cooper girl who whispered back an answer. Sister Nagle hit the Cooper girl with the end of a feather duster which, when it came down, made an eerie whispering sound.

The lesson was begun. Sister Nagle's breasts danced quavers as she conducted. It was held to be difficult, except in her case, to detect bosom under habit, and so the children assumed her to have a disease.

As Mother de Bosco had vetoed other buildings, class was being held in the old school room. For once, Sister Nagle was in agreement. There were more flowers in that part of the schoolyard, and the gardener, her enemy, preferred to concentrate on the front of the school. Moreover she had that wonderful sense of being an artist in exile; and, as she herself acknowledged, of making dangerous bits of glass, her pupils, form into a cathedral window to be envied and admired by parents and the other invitees of an élite musical fraternity at the end of year concert.

'Put expression in your voices,' she reproached. 'You sound dead. I can see your wooden hearts in my spiritual eye. Sing up.'

Although Lucy liked singing, she was beset by a desire to caricature the only nun who favoured her, to test the limits of her own worth. She wondered whether she would get as many red marks on her knuckles as the Cooper girl. If she only got one hit, the latter would be jealous and upset. If she got a severe thrashing, she might not have to pay to be victim next time. Without further contemplation, she began to stretch her face into pious shapes, taunting misdirections, until:

'Lucy Stapleton. Come out to the front please.'

Lucy held her hands behind her back, rubbing them in anticipation of pain.

'That, my dear, was beautiful. Beautiful. So expressive. You remind me of one of my old Eisteddfod pupils. Please, you may take over the singing today. Use my baton.'

Greeting this strange reversal of fate stoically, Lucy began to conduct. There was justice in the world, she thought, but it was often mismanaged. As she conducted, she winked at Adelaide, and whilst pretending to encourage Suzie and Mavis to sing, pulled horrible faces at them.

'You're marvellous, Lucy,' whispered Adelaide. 'Sister

Nagle must pet you. And can I plait your hair after school? It's getting so long.'

Each day the rosary was said. It was a precaution against the daily round of sinning, taken, like milk, to line the stomach.

Mother de Bosco counted her beads with a degree of spiritual rapacity as she paced the aisles of the small brick classroom. Her footsteps sounded heavy and measured in the children's ears. Like a peasant she invoked the black constancy of her beads, praying perhaps that her tally would always remain the same.

Poor Mother, thought Lucy, she must be suffocating in her serge today. Her skin is being pinched by her coif again. The weather is getting so hot and she is trapped inside her black cage. Nobody gets to see her underwear, and her habit is never hanging up to dry. The convent courtyard must be full of washing; full of corsets like cricket pads heavy on the line, laden with hooks and eyes; and those strange darned stockings giving the appearance of misshapen legs dragged across gravel.

Nuns were full of mystery she continued to think, that was why God had chosen them. They were old, closer in their journey to God. Yet they were such a long way from baptism. It was a mystery.

Saints could be any age. In fact they were often very young when they were put to death; few died from old age. Lucy considered that it would be better to qualify for sainthood by being a lay missionary. Nuns were closer to God's toenails. Missionaries were His hands. Both were necessary, but there was no question in Lucy's mind as to which she would rather be.

'According to the teachings of Saint Augustine,' said Mother de Bosco, her words, like toothpicks, picking out the gaps in her teeth, 'people have different capacities for happiness and reward. Some have the capacity of a thimble, and others, a bucket. The thimble has no knowledge of what he is missing, provided he is full to the brim, and the bucket, of course, has a greater quantity of happiness. This is why our heavenly rewards differ, because people have different capacities, and at the same time, some deserve greater endowment.'

Lucy realised at once that her greatest danger lay in being a half-filled bucket. To fail at becoming a saint might mean damnation, or at the very least, the sound of hollow tin ringing through eternity, reminding her of what was missing.

If she had to choose, she would die by little fine arrows that spilled only tendrils of blood. Or better still, she could die one of those rare natural deaths like Saint Margaret Mary who saw the sacred heart burning. What bad luck to be an occasion of sin and get paraded naked like Lady Godiva. Through no fault of her own she had to give up a full bucket in heaven. Fortunately, Saint Catherine (bound to a spiked wheel) had kept a proportion of her clothes on in the process of execution, and she was safe.

Disregarding the haphazard patterns of Lucy's thoughts, the sun was inching its way cautiously to its zenith in the Five Dock sky. Few had noticed its progress that day, except one of the verandah nuns dying of cancer. Some of the children believed that facial cysts were the outward signs of disease. Many of the older nuns had them. Adelaide observed that the verandah nun was always smiling because she wanted to die with a smile on her face, to meet God. Teresa, with the sausage curls, had said that that was a most unsafe way to die, and that it would be better to die with rosary beads clasped to her breast, like Sister Assumpta, who, when the children had paraded past her corpse, was as grim and green as they could have wished.

Cicadas were making a constant lunchtime noise in the playground. This was considered presumptuous for early spring, but the children took for granted they would soon be in boxes, shoeboxes punched with holes, and filled with dead insects. Their constant croaking noise seemed to justify the constancy of dark black prisons. But nothing, absolutely nothing, justified Wayne Thompson, who raced them after he had pulled off their wings.

Adelaide and Lucy sat together as they ate lunch. It was mission day. Every Friday was a mission day. Each week the children were encouraged to bring toffees, and games of chance, to raise money to send to the missionaries whose skins used to turn yellow taking in so much quinine.

'Damn,' said Adelaide furiously. 'Mum's put pickle in my sandwich again. How many times do I have to tell her? My breath's going to smell like the vomit on the floor of that new cheese shop.'

'What,' said Lucy, 'the one that's opened in Haberfield?'

'Where else, it's your suburb,' said her friend, out of humour. 'My mother says it's a shame about the Italians. The whole suburb is going to smell like vomit, and look at the colours they paint their houses, no wonder they vomit, and you can smell it from the bus stop.'

'When I walk past the shop, I just hold my nose,' said Lucy.

'Then do you think I should offer my sandwich to the new Italian girl?'

'I think she's pretty,' said Lucy. 'Her eyes are dark, and she has long graceful arms.'

'Graceful hairy arms,' said Adelaide. 'But I won't have anything to eat if she accepts it.'

'You can have mine,' said Lucy. 'I'm going to buy three toffees today. Dad gave me some money after his big win at Canterbury.'

'I wish my father went to the races,' said Adelaide. 'He

doesn't do anything except re-wire the house, and build a noisy rumpus room so that he can listen to whatever I say from the kitchen.'

'Yes,' said Lucy, 'I know I'm lucky. Dad says you're lucky when you're young, and that's why they made it illegal for young people to bet. The only place I can have a bet is at the picnic races, and the horses are so slow that luck doesn't come into it. Last time I won two shillings.'

'Two shillings?' repeated Adelaide, hoping it wasn't true.

'You can ask my father if you don't believe me,' said Lucy. 'But I had to bet one and six to get it. Dad says the odds are shorter than the jockeys in the country, and Grandfather gets angry. Last time he said that he'd rather gamble on the weather than a crooked horse, and when I looked at my horse it was a strange sort of shape.'

As Lucy and Adelaide talked, Wayne Thompson was conducting a lucky dip. There was a long queue. His goods were known to be of a high quality. Swapping began once the little parcels were opened. There was a good deal of surprise when Wayne suddenly took up the box and went over to the two girls.

'Lucy,' he said, sucking generous portions of air through the gaps in his teeth, 'you can have one of my lucky dips, for nothing. And seeing as though Adelaide is with you, she can have one for half price.'

'No thanks,' said the two girls in unison.

'But I've got some Phantom comics in my dip,' he said, 'and so as people won't recognise them, I've enclosed a note attached to a stone which says "You are the lucky winner of a Phantom No. 23 series!"'

'I don't read Phantom comics,' said Adelaide, looking at him with a mixture of suspicion and haughtiness. 'He can't fly. He can't do anything except get washed up on beaches, and his suit's been growing on him like a mould. He's just fungus features, like you. Lucy doesn't read comics either. She only reads books. Books that you wouldn't understand. So go away, she's my friend, not yours.'

'Yes, that's right. I am,' said Lucy. 'But I may as well try a lucky dip. Being your friend shouldn't stop that.'

Wayne was delighted. He held up the huge decorated box which was full of parcels. Lucy put her hand into the new-smelling shapes, and Wayne tried to grab hold of it. She pulled quickly away.

'I've got something,' she said.

'I can tell,' said Wayne disappointed. 'It's a Phantom comic.' He had hoped they were better disguised.

'No it isn't,' said Lucy joyfully. 'It's a paper lantern, and it's the most beautiful thing I've ever seen. Look. It folds out like an accordion.'

Lucy smiled at Wayne, at the lantern's delicate paintwork, at the spattering of gold lettering telling of another country.

'That woman's got knitting needles through her hair,' said Adelaide. 'She's got a bun stuffed with knitting. Her poor baby is going to have hair all over its booties.'

'She's Japanese,' said Lucy, 'and that's the way they do their hair. My Dad said he would've fought them, if the war office had allowed.'

'My Dad fought the Japs,' said Wayne eagerly. 'He told the war office that he wouldn't let anybody down. He told me how hard it was to see the whites of their eyes, which were mean and slitted like bayonets.'

'What's the advantage of seeing the whites of their eyes?' asked Lucy, extremely curious.

'Don't be stupid Lucy,' said Adelaide. 'If you can see the whites of your enemies' eyes, it means that they're brave, and there's been no crying. You get red eyes when you cry.'

'I know,' said Lucy. 'I know. But I still think the Japanese women are beautiful. They can leave off the men because of the war, but there's no need to leave off the women.'

'Just because you're one,' said Wayne.

'No. It's just that when I think about the Haberfield ladies, especially the ones on the Red Cross stall, I'm glad they didn't paint them.'

'That's a joke,' said Wayne, trying to stamp on a slow-moving fly. 'I bought the lantern from the Red Cross stall. How did you find out?'

'Saints know everything,' said Adelaide.

'And she knew about my cuttlefish bone.'

'What are you going to do for the missions, Lucy?' they asked.

'If I'm a saint,' said Lucy, 'then I'm going to pray. My mother doesn't approve of toffees. She says that missionaries don't need them.'

'Does she approve of chocolate crackles?' Adelaide asked.

'No,' she said, 'but it doesn't matter, because one day I'm going to be a missionary myself. And then people will have to make toffees and chocolate crackles for me. And when I've finished being a missionary I'm going over to Ireland to be canonised.'

'But how can you be good enough to be a saint,' said Wayne, 'when Mother de Bosco isn't?'

'My father,' returned Lucy, contemptuously, 'says that anyone can be anything, provided they're in the right place at the right time. Mother de Bosco is in Australia, but if she were in Ireland, she'd be made a saint immediately.'

'Shouldn't she be a greater saint for staying in Australia in order to deny herself?' asked Adelaide, with legal cunning.

'She should,' said Lucy respectfully, 'but as you know, there have to be some good people to guide out the wicked, and this country is full of wickedness. My mother says it's like an oven without a thermostat.'

'I don't think it's fair,' said Wayne, 'that Mother de Bosco has to stay in Australia and lose her chance of becoming a saint. I'd like to see her being flayed alive, like Saint Bartholomew was.'

'Her skin's so loose,' said Lucy, rather regretfully. It would be such an easy task. 'I'm going to start perishing slowly in the desert,' she continued. 'Then, as I'm perishing, I'll request to be sent back to Ireland to die. They won't be able to refuse.'

'Can I plait your hair, Lucy?' said Wayne, taking advantage of her mood of sentimentality. 'I've been practising on my sister.'

'No,' she said, 'boys hurt when they plait. But I'll let you brush it, now that you've given me this lantern.'

As soon as Wayne had left, Adelaide began to dance on the faded bitumen that was the basketball court. Full of stern animation and a no-nonsense cuteness, she addressed Lucy sharply:

'I know why he wants to play with you,' she said, with her adult lack of curiosity. 'He's a half-price rat. Everybody knows that.'

'He's trying to improve,' said Lucy. 'He doesn't hang around the toilets so much. And Suzie likes him now, even if Mavis doesn't.'

'He's disgusting,' said her friend. 'And you'd better watch out because my mother says you're maleable.'

'What's maleable?' Lucy asked.

'It means you change, from one male to the next.'

'But I don't play with boys,' said Lucy righteously.

'You'll go changing,' said Adelaide.

'Well I don't care,' said Lucy. 'Saint Augustine went bad before he went good. He was maleable.'

'If he was anything,' said Adelaide, 'he was femaleable, and going from one female to the next. But that isn't possible, because there's no such word as femaleable.

Only females can be maleable.'

Adelaide had won the argument. Lucy had the paper lantern. Both were reasonably happy with the arrangement, until Lucy began chewing a sticture toffee, and it refused to budge.

The toffee gripped her teeth like a vice. Friends and enemies united in their aid. Hands pulled at mouth, elbows jammed against her jaws. Nobody saw any humour in a toffee turned inhospitable. Every variety of ingenuity was called for and every consideration of treachery made. It was an affront to the stability of the dull dusty yard to have what appeared to be a natural disaster in their midst.

'I bet your mother made the toffee, Wayne Thompson,' said Adelaide, searching to find someone safe on whom to lay the blame.

'No. Not me,' he said. 'I only brought in the lucky dip. Mrs Sillon made it. I saw her with it when she dropped John at school this morning.'

'You're a great liar,' said Mavis. 'Mrs Sillon made the green ones with hundreds and thousands.' She went over to him and pulled his ears with her toffee fingers. He screamed in pain. 'But we all know that you wouldn't do anything to your girlfriend. Bad luck she's all glued up. Bad luck for you.'

'Kiss your girlfriend now,' said someone else, pleased to be diverted from the real calamity. 'Oh, sorry. I meant lick your girlfriend.'

'Be quiet,' said Teresa angrily. She was strengthened by the sight of suffering.

'And leave Wayne Thompson alone,' said Adelaide.

Lucy grunted.

'She wants something,' said one of the younger boys. 'She's trying to tell us something.'

'Paw it on the ground,' said one of the very young, 'like a horse.'

'Grunt it out in morse code,' said Wayne. 'My brother taught me morse code.'

Lucy's large eyes grew larger with pleading.

'Can't you grunt?' said Adelaide. 'Like this.'

There were many on hand to demonstrate various techniques. In desperation Lucy dismissed them violently with her arm movements.

'She wants us to go and get Mother,' said Teresa.

Lucy shook her head violently, but it was rather a redundant gesture, as Mother de Bosco had arrived.

'What's this?' she asked with generous brutality. Like most people she preferred the rhetorical question. 'You can come with me to the convent. I'll fix you up.'

Lucy put her hand in her blazer pocket to check if her lantern was still there. Then she reluctantly followed the black bentness of her teacher into the convent.

In the huge kitchen a nun was baking biscuits. She offered one of them to Lucy with a half smile on her face.

'That'll do, Sister. Has the floor polish arrived yet? We're running low. Look at this child. What a lesson in self-indulgence. This kitchen will take two coats. Don't worry dear, we'll have it fixed in no time. We all need a mouth, don't we?'

Mother de Bosco placed an enormous kettle on the wood stove. Lucy was so surprised to see her teacher in a kitchen, let alone taking time to relax and make herself a cup of tea, she decided to relax herself.

The other nun left. Her habit was hitched up, revealing two muscular stumps and black orthopaedic shoes.

'This'll take care of things,' said Mother de Bosco, pouring boiling water into a cup. 'We'll just have to melt the toffee.'

Before Lucy could grunt out surprise, the hot water was thrown onto her mouth.

'It's starting to melt already,' said her teacher. 'But I suspect it'll take a while. Don't worry, dear. God will give you strength. Don't move.'

Lucy went down on her knees to weep.

'The difference between saints and ordinary people,' said Mother de Bosco, 'is the way saints embrace suffering, and death, like a lover. Sit on the chair and keep still.'

She settled over Lucy like a black hen.

'What if Mother has got a taste for shell,' Lucy thought to herself. Grandfather had told her about those hens. Once eggshell was left in their scraps they got a taste for eating their own eggs.

He used to tell her every time she visited that there was a special tin for hen scraps and a special tin for eggshell. No one could forget, he said, how closely protection and destruction were allied. The two tins were a useful reminder.

When Mother de Bosco's task was accomplished, Lucy was sent home red-mouthed, blistered, with a note to her parents. Her mother would probably not be sympathetic. She didn't approve of toffees. Her father might laugh, if his humour was up to it. Otherwise he would tell her about life, and how she was lucky the toffee had been freed without the help of local anaesthetic, how resourceful the nuns were, how they had given him the cane when he was at school, how underneath it all he was grateful they had been strict with him, given him a sense of responsibility, made him into a man even before the brothers had had their chance.

It was no use talking to parents. They soaked up misfortune like a sponge, and never did anything about it. She pulled her panama hat low over her face, hoping no one would see her mouth.

She walked quickly past the bus stop, the banksia, and a blockful of Federation houses. The houses had a way of playing with light to make it look solid. The street was a paragon of dull respectability. The first garden estate, project home village in Sydney. It had been built on an area where flatness should have invited industry.

As Lucy walked past the Red Cross stall, with its jams, aprons, coathangers and second-hand books, one of the women looked closely at her mouth.

'That's the Stapleton girl, isn't it?' she said, gluing a label to a jar of plum jam. 'Her poor mother. Not a bad type really. Joe Ryan says he takes the bets.'

'Good luck to Joe then,' said another, 'if she's stupid enough to allow her husband to bet. The girl takes after her father, apparently. But she hasn't got his looks.'

'If it wasn't for the way her mouth seems to be growing, I'd say she'd be all right.'

'A mouth's important,' said her friend. 'Mrs Swanton's daughter was ruined by her mouth.'

'Wasn't it the girl's teeth,' said the other, 'pushing her face out? She used to remind me of a fish with its mouth full of coral. And that reminds me, Coral's had a miscarriage.'

'Miscarriage!' they exclaimed, too old to be in unison. 'Misc.' 'Carriage.'

When Lucy arrived home she dropped the note into her mother's lap and began to cry.

'Read it,' she said. 'It's about my ugly old mouth.'

'It was an adequate mouth this morning,' said her mother. 'What's happened?'

'Read it. I've got to go to my room.'

Lucy ran sobbing into her bedroom. She placed her crucifix cross-beam to the coloured light shed by her windows. They were church windows. Sometimes their light would bend across her fireplace like a wand.

She looked at her mouth in the mirror. It had a tight slimy gloss, like a sheep's organ spilled on the slaughterhouse floor.

Poor ugly mouth. It might never look the same again. The only consolation was that God favoured mutilation. She cried louder, recalling a story that Mother had told them about a beautiful nun in Germany during the Second World War.

In those days, soldiers were billeted at convents, nursed by the nuns when necessary. There was one nun so beautiful that she had looked soft and shapely, even in a nun's habit.

A certain soldier during convalescence found himself drawn to her striking beauty. He was lonelier and more impious than the rest and so began to touch the shy nun.

Touching, looking, begging. Each day his attentions grew stronger, until one day he had to confess his dreams to her. He told her how he was wet and weakened by desire, how he couldn't even go to confession because he would sin again the very next day. Every day he sinned, whispering a new doubt into her small ears. And with every day a resolution formed itself strongly in her mind.

She took a knife from the kitchen and plucked out one of her eyes.

No longer a temptation, an occasion of sin, she had saved her own soul at least. For while she had tempted the soldier, she herself had been sinning mortally. The source of sin, like the source of a river, was inseparable from the flow.

The pretty little nun thus became proud of her disfigurement. It guaranteed her spiritual safety. The soldier grew to respect the person he had once merely desired. And in remembrance of her victory, she used to wear her black eye-patch with a relic of Saint Agnes stitched into its lining.

That was how God favoured mutilation. The plucking out of eyes, mouths. The only problem was, He had had to pluck out her mouth for her. Telling her she was too slow in going about her sainthood. Mother de Bosco had said she was slow.

What if she were being punished for talking about babies, and how mothers could bleed to death when they menstruated?

Doubts, like the plantar warts on the Cooper girl's feet, began to proliferate in her mind. Saints didn't wait for things to happen. They had a heightened sense of free will. In mutilation and opposition, they were God's vandals. She did nothing. She was nothing. She had been too full of her own importance, and only the nun in the story had reason to be proud.

Looking at her mouth, touching it delicately, she examined the full extent of her deformity. It raised many questions in her mind, questions never raised before.

What if the death process, like the birth, produced mistakes? What if she found herself unable to sing in heaven because of a hare-lip, deformed mouth?

Would she be caesarian in her death, as she had been at birth? Her mother was always telling everyone how she'd been cut open to have her baby.

But worse, much worse, could she die a Siamese twin? Attached to a damned partner, crying out her innocence into a black abyss while they were both thrown onto flames?

'God,' she prayed desperately to herself. 'Make me into a normal dead spirit. Don't be impatient, or tear me too roughly out of life. There is an eternity of time to be filled in, an eternity of time.'

Lying on her bed, she crushed an ant between her fingers, making it into a black ball to smell. Grandfather had fine red veins on the side of his forehead. She was growing pubic hair.

On Sundays, poor Christ would have to come inside her blistered puffy mouth with its full set of yellow teeth. The world was a dark place, and she had only the merest paper lantern on which to rely.

4

    Shine little glow-worm, glitter, glitter.
    Shine little glow-worm, glitter, glitter.
    Lead us lest too far we wander.
    Love's sweet voice is calling yonder.

The class weaved in figure of eight formation across the stage. They were holding their torches, which, on the night of the concert, would shine various colours into the darkness.

Most of them had expressed approval of Sister Nagle's idea, as none had seen a glow-worm before. The irradiated nematode held a fascination for them. It was far more interesting than being the huntsmen and pansies of previous years.

'Leave off, Mary. Can't you see your torch is burning into the back of my neck.' Adelaide, less than all of them, wanted to be a glow-worm. 'I think this has gone far enough,' she continued, grafting indignation onto her innate contempt for frivolity. 'My mother's paid a fortune for my costume material and my birthday is next week. I bet I don't get as good a present. She spends all her time making up my costume, and I don't even get afternoon tea now, after school.'

'Shut up, Adelaide,' said Teresa, her sausage curls shaking violently. These eight neat tubes of hair were a barometer of the young girl's emotions; they spoke her conscience. The other children rarely defied them.

'All right, Teresa,' said Adelaide, her voice now steady. 'I'm just feeling sorry for the mothers, and all the work they have to do.'

The school hall was not used frequently. It had an insufficient number of windows. It couldn't accommodate large crowds without claiming a number of dizzy fainting victims. Nevertheless it had been deemed acceptable for the end of year concert, as no other alternative was available.

By virtue of a total lack of interest, the school hall had become a shrine to Sister Nagle's musical triumphs. And, as is the case with most 'annuals', a brighter and more variegated show of colour was hoped for with each spring planting.

There was something about a public occasion which genuinely frightened Sister Nagle, living as she did in the seclusion of a convent. But it was that fear which made it all worthwhile. In a convent, frailty had to be dress rehearsed before it was placed in the darkness and privacy of a confessional. Ideally, a public stage should resemble a confessional, or an open coffin, where something final and good could be said about its contents. Should the corpse move, violating the natural law, fear and judgement would be let loose upon the audience. The corpse would be trampled in the rush to escape. There must be no mistakes. She would rehearse those children until they became fixed in time and faultless as if they were dead.

As the day grew nearer, she began a painting campaign of unparalleled munificence. However, it had to be admitted that some of the children were disappointed with the results. Several hydrangeas at the hall's entrance had been painted pink and mauve. They viewed these concessions to nature and naturalism as cowardice, and symptomatic of Mother de Bosco's increasing influence in the school.

There was little doubt that the dingy red-brick hall was more in keeping with other buildings in Five Dock. The older convent block, with its mixture of Dublin and

France, its tentative lace handkerchief roof, was out of place. Perhaps the roof had been thrown over, in those early days, to make peace not merely with the various architectural styles within the building, but with the suburb as a whole.

Certainly the hall was in tune with the rest of Five Dock. Seeming, like other buildings in the suburb, to be floating on its own independent lake of heat. Floating, a scum of red brick, across something unexplored. Any heavier, and the building, civilisation with it, might sink. The ecology of the flat, unwholesome land forbade ambition.

'The Archbishop will be coming,' Sister Nagle told the children. 'And there will be a large musical fraternity present. I am placing my trust in you, my little worms, to guide your wandering audience to bliss. Bliss is blessed. Listen to the music of those words. God is music. I have often wanted, without being able, to paint crotchets on my flowers. Crotchets and quavers, and sweet dotted minims.'

'What's she talking about?' asked one of the children.

'I don't know,' replied Wayne Thompson. 'She's crazy. Even Mother de Bosco says that.' His bus ticket was wet with chewing-saliva. He always waited for something to destroy before throwing it away.

'Well I've got an idea,' said his friend. 'I was thinking about it last night.'

'What?'

'You know what?'

'What?'

'We. You and me.' He adopted the sycophantic demeanour of a mate. 'You and I. Why don't we swap batteries? Dead ones for new ones on the night of the concert. Then, there'd be all this music, all the shine little glow-worm, and we'd come on to the stage with our torches, and there'd be no light, and Sister Nagle would have a heart attack, and an ambulance would come. We'd only leave one battery, just one.'

'Why just one battery?' asked Wayne, captivated.

'So Sister Nagle will have someone to suspect. God you're stupid sometimes. The obvious person to suspect is the one with the good torch.'

'But she'll sniff a frame-up, won't she?'

'Why?'

'I don't know, but I suppose she's going to suspect us.'

'Why?' his friend repeated. 'We can leave Mavis with the torch. I want to pay her back for my tadpoles. I've only got one left.'

'What about the Italian?' suggested Wayne. 'He won't pay you back like Mavis. And he's got greasy hair, greasy like spaghetti fat.'

'But Mavis deserves it more.'

'But Mavis is not Italian,' Wayne insisted. 'And her father plays bowls. Next year they're going to elect him president of the club.'

'Well,' said his friend gravely, 'I've seen Mavis without her pants on. She's got black hairs all over her body, like a forest.'

'But she's not Italian. I know she's not.'

'Then if that's what she's like,' his friend intimated mysteriously, 'what about Claudio? He must be a sight.'

'It'd be like being a prisoner,' said Wayne, 'like being a prisoner in your own hair, all trapped up in black wire.'

'And not even Houdini could escape from that sort of prison,' agreed his friend. 'Harry Houdini, or "Hairy" to his friends.'

For the remainder of the rehearsal the two boys proposed victims, placing them in a crude order of merit. In the heat names were repeated. Rehearsed. It was a rehearsal. And if Sister Nagle achieved her ends, the word could be broken down into its component parts. Re-hearse-all.

'My costume prickles,' said Lucy, on the night of the concert.

'It shouldn't,' said her mother. 'The nuns chose the most expensive material they could find. They only take a vow of poverty for themselves.'

'What if, tonight,' asked Lucy, 'I have to scratch my nose while I'm holding my torch?'

'Too bad,' interrupted her father, never at his best on family occasions. 'How do you think we feel, having to sit through the whole thing.'

'It's only one night,' said Lucy's mother. But the narrow possibilities suggested by this *only* increased her bitterness. She continued more harshly. 'Ever since your father bought his television, he hasn't wanted to go anywhere.'

'Tell me then,' he said, 'where would you like me to go?' Before she could make the obvious reply, the reply he expected, he resumed. 'Harold Park? I thought you'd be grateful for something that kept me home.'

'No,' she said, 'I'm afraid not.'

'Then tell me why Joe Ryan hasn't got a television. With all his money. We're the pioneers. We're the real pioneers.'

'No pioneers ever paid what we had to pay for our television set. Pioneers do their pioneering on a shoestring.'

'Half the street has asked me if they can come over tonight, to watch. There are some good programmes tonight.'

'You can stay home if you want, Dad,' said Lucy, 'as long as Mum comes.'

'That's all right,' he said ungraciously, 'I'll come. I want to get as much mileage out of that worm suit of yours as I can. By ghost it was expensive. I've had to recoup by betting on which one of you children is going to fall over. I said to one of the fathers that nobody's taken into account that your rehearsals have all been during the day.'

'I can't see properly in this costume,' said Lucy, frightened. 'It might be going to be me.'

'No chance,' he said. 'The Stapletons are sure-footed.' He blinked back the surprise he felt at his own confidence. 'And I've had a win today.'

'Then you don't need me to fall over tonight?' asked Lucy anxiously. 'You don't need the money?'

Her father laughed loudly, as if he were outside. There was often something disproportionate about him. A jockey grown too tall, he had been cheated of the living he had hoped to gamble away.

They were eating dinner. His good looks were least efficacious at meal times. He had a bad set of false teeth which clinked mechanically as he ate. When sitting at the table he appeared like a fastidious doll, or an effigy with a limited number of movements.

'Leave it to someone else to fall over,' he said, dropping a dollop of potato in his lap and scooping it quickly back up on to his plate.

'We learnt a psalm about slipping,' Lucy said, thinking of David in his royal slippers. Even kings could worry about such things and play of them upon their harps:

'For I said: Let not mine enemies at any time triumph over me; and when my feet slip they have spoken great things against me. For I am prepared for scourges and my sorrow is always before me.'

'I've stitched your feeler on upside down,' said her mother, cramped and exasperated by her efforts.

'It might be the Cooper girl,' said Lucy. 'Her mother is buying her new shoes, and they're always slippery. Slipper-y. I hadn't thought about the way that word breaks down. And Sister Nagle is going to polish the floor into glass.'

'Keep still,' said her mother. 'They spend a fortune on the costume material, then economise on the feelers.

Ridiculous. They're limp and crushed already, and I haven't even finished stitching them.'

'I don't see why Sister Nagle wants feelers,' said Lucy, glumly. 'Worms don't have them, do they?'

'It's for the effect,' laughed her mother.

'But what's the use when they burrow all day. Butterflies might need them, but worms wouldn't.'

'But you're special,' she said, affectionately pulling her daughter's antennae. 'You're glow-worms.'

'But a worm's feelers would be crushed every time it burrowed.'

'Worms can't see,' said her mother, 'so they might be grateful for a set.'

'Sister Nagle told us that they have to glow to compensate for their blindness, that they have special powers to lead others. They can guide people back to their friends and family. The blind humble worm will lead lovers back to the path of righteousness. It's a mystery, and natural mysteries reflect divine.'

'Yes that's right,' said her mother. 'Nature leads us to God.'

She placed a shovelful of coal into their cosy stove. It was summer and she had no intention of lighting it.

'I hope your father wears his dark suit tonight. All the men will be in something dark.'

'Your husband,' he replied, 'will wear his pale blue suit.'

'And I suppose,' said Mrs Stapleton, 'that if she's prepared to paint flowers, she's . . . I just wish that she hadn't economised on the feelers.'

'Your husband will wear his pale blue suit,' he repeated firmly.

'Good then,' she said bitterly. 'When everyone else is in black, we'll look like the criminal and his mother dressed sharply to get up an alibi.'

'Pull your finger out,' he said. 'You're out of place in

Five Dock because you can't get along with the people. That's your problem. Don't blame that on the way I dress.'

'No,' she said. 'There's nothing I want to blame on you, nothing.'

'Good,' he said, with little satisfaction. 'I'll turn off the television.'

Splashing into the watery darkness, the Stapletons' Holden made its way to Five Dock. Lucy watched her parents. Her father seemed to be leaning too heavily on the wheel, like a council worker resting on his shovel with an indolent determination to do as little work as possible. The corners of her mother's eyes were wet. Beautiful eyes, emphasised in the traffic by red, green, a fan of white headlamp and the constant particled fluorescence of street light. She turned round towards Lucy and smiled anxiously.

'You're a pretty glow-worm tonight,' she said. 'Pinch your cheeks and they'll go pink. I'll put some lipstick on you when we get there.'

Lucy partook eagerly in this conspiracy of beauty, looking across to her father whose shaven neck had a prickly scoured surface with no suggestion of a handsome face on the other side. Behind the wheel he looked a veritable Janus, a two-faced god stuck behind a steering column. He cut everyone down to size with his unpredictable mediocrity. Inanities poured from the face she couldn't see, the handsome face abusing its fellow drivers, commenting on the occasional blonde, and showing its coarse neck and brilliantine to her.

Yet she felt confident about her father, possibly she loved him. For he had an admirable disregard for social acceptance. His gambling, in its limited way, gave him the independence of a saint. In her world of strange and exclusive sacrifice he was a martyr, a martyr by default, who lost his friends, gambled his pleasure away for the sake of some indefinable reward. Saint Peter had asked to be crucified upside down. Her father, selfish, mechanical, pockets tipped outwards, and oblivious, lived in that shadow.

Lucy felt that her mother, in spite of a redoubtable profile, was to be pitied. She was vulnerable, reacting to people as if they were about to hit her. And just as she seemed to love her daughter, she spent much of her time teaching her how to minister to failure.

When they arrived, the concert hall had a yellowish glow which went well enough with the nuns' habits and with those men who had chosen to wear dinner suits.

Lucy felt grown up, especially when she observed the child-like complacency affected by some of the parents. The stage seemed a sanctuary to her, like the temples of ancient Greece, where she and the others were high priests, immune from the commune at large. The nuns looked nervous in the special wooden chairs they had had brought from the convent.

The Five Dock hall was an unmixed cocktail of builders, tradesmen, clerks and policemen spilled over the furniture. Several mothers had made cautious territorial gains over the aluminium chairs. Some had straight skirts creeping over their knees, with their suspenders outlined and ineffectual in the fight against ankle-sagging nylon. Other mothers wore full skirts which looped like rope over the unshaven down of their legs. Mrs Stapleton dressed plainly. Neat, glum and muscular, she suggested the country town rather than the declining squatocracy she'd been born into.

'Is that your daughter up there with Adelaide Booth?' asked Mrs Thompson, curious to see the girl her son admired, who had caused him to throw away his cuttlefish bone.

'Yes,' said Mrs Stapleton. 'And you can see that she looks like her father. She's a year too old for her class.'

'Is she?' said Mrs Thompson, with no curiosity in her voice. 'So is Wayne. But I have to laugh at the crush he has on her. Every day he comes home with some little story.'

'Yes,' repeated Mrs Stapleton, pausing before a rush of words came out. Sensing an imminent landslide, her companion intervened:

'My husband is trying to get onto the local council.'

'I think we'll need him if they're going to dredge the harbour,' said Mrs Stapleton politely. 'Half a million pounds for the dredging equipment. It's a lot of money to spend to get rid of low tide, I mean the smell of low tide. It's a lot of money to spend on a smell.'

'You're right of course,' interrupted Mrs Thompson. 'I find it very good that Merv has his politics,' she said, emphasising the courtesy of continuing with the subject. 'It's like the Masons, it keeps him away from women.'

'Perhaps.' Mrs Stapleton attempted to laugh. 'But I didn't think Catholics could become Masons.'

'A shibbolith,' said Mrs Thompson, using a word which conjured anti-semitism rather than any other prejudice. 'There are plenty of doors open to Catholics these days. They just have to overcome their stigmata.'

'Really,' said Mrs Stapleton, wondering what it would be like to be a politician's wife. All she had known about Merv Thompson until now was that he played bowls and kept bees.

'I must go over and talk to Mother de Bosco,' said Mrs Thompson with the broad charming smile of a first lady. 'She's done some embroidery for me. I haven't got the patience,' she said imploringly. 'And tell Lucy that I think she looks beautiful tonight. She really is a pretty girl, and children recognise these things, don't they? I'll see you at supper Mrs Stapleton.'

No you won't. No you won't. There was an intransigence about Mrs Stapleton that seemed to counteract her desire for friends. Perhaps she was growing too old, perhaps the lines on her face had become the deep stubborn scars of a slave that could not be ministered to by any heavy-handed Hollywood beauty like Mrs Thompson. What she really yearned for was a spark of compassion, a spark in someone's gaze which she could eagerly and nobly extinguish. But the eyes she met were calloused, glazed and pickled, flitting like fleas in their eye sockets. It was her fault for marrying the wrong man. If only she could be back in the country and free from her choice.

Backstage, Wayne Thompson was enjoying the imprisonment of his worm suit. His feelers were bent like rabbit ears, lending him the stereotyped innocence of childhood. He wanted to parade his cuteness, but wasn't sure how to go about it. In the end he settled upon the strident fellowship of the mouseketeer, recently presented on his neighbour's television set.

'Well,' said his friend aggressively, 'did you bring the batteries?'

'No I didn't,' said Wayne. 'It was a stupid idea.'

'I always knew that you were a yellow-bellied taipan.'

'No I'm not,' said Wayne, impressed by the conspiracy of circumstance. 'I'm a worm. Ha. Ha. I'm a worm.'

'You just couldn't find enough dead batteries, could you?'

'Why should I?'

'And where's your mother?' asked his friend.

'Where's yours?'

'Behind the Bishop, in the third row,' said his friend.

'And your poor mother is right at the back of the hall. Ha. Ha. Dressed in that pink sparkly stuff.'

'Sister Nagle said we would at least get an archbishop. It might be worth sitting behind one of them.'

'It doesn't make any difference,' said his friend. 'They are all God's servants.'

'Oh yes it does. An archbishop is equal to a butler, and a bishop is only worth a maid. One's a Lord and the other's a Grace. And the ladder works like our missal. You have the bishop who is equal to a cherubim in heaven, the archbishop who's a seraphim, and the cardinal who's equal to an archangel.'

'Shouldn't an archbishop equal an archangel?' asked his friend suspiciously. 'That'd make more sense.'

'No,' said Wayne firmly. 'It's a mystery, and mysteries don't have to.'

The stagelights dimmed. Blackness. The children giggled, pushed, and touched one another in illicit places.

'Stop that.'

'Get out.'

'Ssh.'

'Quiet.'

'My torch is flickering.'

'Line up.'

'Sister Nagle said she'd give the signal.'

'No. Don't go out now. Not now.'

One bar early, the trail of glow-worms twinkled with intrepid brilliance on to the stage. Every arm was released out of its costume to hold a torch with a different coloured light filtering through cellophane. It was a planetarium of patterned colour that none, not even the discerning Sister Nagle, could fault.

The audience clapped enthusiastically, except for the nuns in the first two rows, who all abstained.

Mrs Stapleton was pleased with the performance. A

school concert, owing to the special patronage of its audience, could confer a warmth. In many respects it was a command performance, at which the nuns and the parents were given priority over the box office and all forms of crude commercialism. The emphasis was on the family. The tasteless furs and joyless glitter of the audience could be both embraced and excused, according to the principles of an exclusive society, until the lights went on.

Mrs Stapleton, proud of her daughter, was nevertheless disturbed by the quality of stubborn grace which the stage seemed to be accentuating in her. Her child had never been obedient, or even child-like. There seemed to be no hope of her looking cute like some of the other worms. She was like her father, full of lazy hope. She would be extremely lucky to find a husband. What institution would accept the crumbs of co-operation she offered? And yet, she was likeable enough, in the way that all daughters are who have their futures before them.

'Mother de Bosco, it was absolutely beautiful,' said Mrs Stapleton, not realising her *faux pas*. 'I particularly liked the Santa Lucia.'

'Sister Nagle's done a wonderful job' said the nun harshly. 'Let there be no mistake about that.'

'And how is Lucy getting along at school? I meant to answer your last note, but I've been going back and forth from the country, and as Lucy's probably told you, I've just had my veins done.'

'Your veins,' said Lucy's teacher with emphasis. 'No. Lucy didn't tell me.'

'How's she going at school anyway?'

'Not very well, I'm afraid. Not very well.'

'Well she's very good when she's in the country,' said Mrs Stapleton apologetically. 'Very good.'

'Well I don't know much about the country,' Mother de Bosco lied. She had been brought up on a small farm, but she convinced herself she was speaking generically, about Australia at large.

'She's too old for her class,' the nun continued. 'Too old emotionally, and intellectually backward.'

'But she has friends,' said Mrs Stapleton.

'So that she can be one better than them all the time.'

'I don't think she'd get the better of Adelaide Booth.'

'This obsession with becoming a saint,' said Mother de Bosco, tactfully, as she dealt with all the small obscenities of life, 'don't you think that it's a little precocious in a backward child? I've tried to interest her in a religious vocation, but to no avail. To put the problem in a nutshell, Mrs Stapleton, she places her faith in the senses rather than in the well-trained intellect. I don't think we'll be able to cope with her next year, when her body starts to change.'

'Then you must tell me what she has done wrong,' said Mrs Stapleton, straightening the damp creases in her dress, preparing herself for a rush of despair.

'She hasn't done anything serious, yet. But we don't want to wait for the eggs of the serpent to hatch, as the saying goes.'

Mrs Stapleton was relieved that Lucy had committed no concrete misdemeanour. It gave her the courage to condemn her daughter and removed the burden of specific defence.

'She reads so much, the poor thing. She must be using it as a smokescreen, in the hope that we won't notice her backwardness. However I can't be too hard on her for that.'

'No, Mrs Stapleton. It is unwise to be too hard on anyone.'

'She's a little sub-normal?' asked Mrs Stapleton.

'I wouldn't say "sub". I would prefer to call her slow. And in theological experience, it is the slow rebels who are dangerous. They are the real force of social decay and spiritual lethargy in society.'

'What can I do?' asked Mrs Stapleton nervously.

'Have you considered another school?'

'No,' replied Mrs Stapleton, shocked. 'No I've never considered another school.'

'That is of course understandable,' said de Bosco, her black pelt glistening in the humidity of the concert hall. 'We keep our standards high.'

'High,' repeated Mrs Stapleton. 'I know. Reg was saying the other day how high your standards were.'

'Which is just the point,' said the nun, looking distastefully at Mrs Stapleton's strapless evening dress cracking away from her like a shell. 'Standards force us to separate the chaff from the grain. We have an obligation to the other parents, as well as to you and your husband. I haven't met your husband, have I?'

'No Mother,' said Mrs Stapleton, returning to her own days as a schoolgirl, sharply reprimanded.

'Obligations have to be met.'

'We'll have to send her to a more expensive school.'

'With prayer . . .' said the nun.

'This school was within our budget . . .'

'All things are possible,' continued de Bosco. 'It's not easy for us either. Enrolments are declining. They're threatening to take away State Aid from us. Let me recommend the family rosary. It is better, Mrs Stapleton, to nip things in the bud. To continue the Shakespearian comparison I used earlier, to kill them in the shell. But you must excuse me, I've promised to go over to the Bishop. God bless you. I'm deeply sorry at the pain I've had to cause.'

Mother de Bosco left Mrs Stapleton, to talk with animation to the Bishop. Her rosary beads rattled like bones by her side. The cerise bonding and lining of the Bishop's vestments were always a welcome display of colour to her, like a show of azaleas at a wedding reception, or the excitement of spring in a council park. She was drawn out of herself by the purple underside of the man, his silk lining, the covered buttons of his grace. Nuns had no comparable underbelly. The tantalising silk was left to the male of the species. That Stapleton woman was a down in the mouth, and what dismal cunning she showed complimenting Sister Nagle in her presence. It went to show how the dullest of dogs could learn tricks. She felt obligated to pray for her.

'What was Mother de Bosco saying?' Lucy asked her mother eagerly. Her costume by this time was torn into a toga.

'Nothing,' said her mother, drawing in a quantity of brittle air. 'Nothing. But what am I going to do with you?'

'John's costume got ripped worse than mine did. You should see his.'

'I'm not talking about your costume,' her mother said, lowering her voice. 'I don't mean that.'

'You said I could ask Adelaide to come up to the country with me.'

'I don't mean that,' her mother repeated.

'Then what have I done?'

'I don't know,' said her mother without enthusiasm. 'It was probably too dreadful for Mother de Bosco to say.'

'I've done nothing dreadful,' said Lucy, 'nothing really dreadful. Is she going to tell you what it is?'

'No,' said her mother, content to let her daughter off the hook.

'Then I've done nothing really dreadful.'

'But she wants you to leave the school.'

'I can't leave the school,' said Lucy stubbornly. 'There's a dog I feed in the playground. It'd starve without me. You should see its ribs, even when I feed it.'

'She has insisted that you leave the school. Unfortunately we'll have to send you somewhere more expensive. We can't really afford it. You see you're a backward learner.'

'Oh,' said Lucy, curious as to what a backward learner was. Her writing went backwards, in spite of the slope card she had to use. It probably meant that she was a bit thick, like Teresa, but that was barely conceivable. What she did like about the description was its unarguable quality, satisfying the more abstract requirements of justice.

'Then I'll go and tell Adelaide,' she said, 'in case she doesn't want to come to the country with me.'

Mrs Stapleton watched the half-peeled worm of her daughter searching for her friend. She didn't really believe Mother de Bosco's diagnosis. She had accused Lucy of subnormality in order to save time, and face, and the parade of petty incidents that would have justified the nun's decision. It was an unpleasant but unavoidable business to lie in co-operation with the forces of authority. But Lucy would probably be much happier in a new school, in a better suburb, like Strathfield, where the mothers would be less like terriers, more like labradors. She could borrow the money from the special fund they kept in the factory. After all, she'd been working there for more than ten years.

Later that night she heard crying from her daughter's bedroom. It was a desperate, relieved kind of sobbing like the breaking of a drought. For Lucy, her end was also the end of Mother de Bosco. She had tried to win that old black nun over, but she had failed. Mother de Bosco was, in effect, dead.

For the first time in her life Lucy felt that she was right in the centre of things. There was a lot to look back over, and an equal amount to surmise. But she would have to be careful, for being backward, time might go too slowly for her. If she improved herself, and studied, and became dutiful, it might go faster. Faster. Her bedclothes drew her into sleep, sleep without nightmares. She was being spared for the waking world, for Adelaide and the country in summer.

Part II

5

Lucy thought back to the dubious days of Mother de Bosco, to the first crisis which, like a first love, couldn't be easily forgotten. Yet de Bosco was dead. God had reluctantly claimed His bride, carried her across the threshold of the underworld, whispering love's sweet litanies into her ancient ears.

Even now the old nun was mentioned in the liturgy, but without the club-footed dignity of Church Latin. Her commemoration was in plain Protestant English. There were now no beguiling accents dangled over the Latin like knife blades for the priest to stumble across in Julius Caesar fashion. The deathlike exhalations of the parish priest assumed importance in Lucy's memory.

'*Memento étiam, Dómine, famulórum famularúmque tuárum Mother de Bosco qui nos praecessérunt cum signo fídei, et dórmiunt in somno pacis.*'

That's what de Bosco should have got. Perhaps she was filing suit right now, making a claim for celestial damages. Perhaps when Lucy died she would have to give evidence on the nun's behalf, delivering an impassioned speech from the dock, telling the court without the need for an oath how Mother de Bosco deserved to be treated with High Mass seriousness, how she'd earned her Latin by the sweat of her brow, not like some, out of privilege. And now after all her struggling the commemoration was in English, a language for heretics.

Lucy thought back to the dramatic pedal pauses and discords in Latin. They were the kind of lightning bolts that had made her jump out of her skin. Those who didn't feel worthy enough to receive the sacrament like herself lived dangerously, committing the sin of 'over-scrupulousness'. This was different from the virtue of humility in a way she'd never quite understood.

Life was full of imponderable paradoxes. Thank God there were concrete realities to look back on, like holy cards. There were 160 interleaved in her missal. Martyrs were always put to death in different ways. They were white skinned for the blood to show pretty, and their eyes looked up to heaven. Banal as comics, they had been part of another time when she'd hoarded, swapped, inspected, bargained over them until they'd become sacred and immutable. She'd brought her favourite one with her for the train. The Annunciation. The idea of an angel coming from heaven to visit with neighbourhood news seemed very gossipy, relaxed. She wished she'd had a card of Gabriel telling Joseph to cross the desert. That would have given her the satisfaction of a precedent.

She had spent many Masses drinking tea with Gabriel. They played tennis together, and when the game was over he would talk delightfully, fanning her with his large soft wings, sometimes allowing her to comb his feathers, or smooth them down to their cloud tips into a suitable angle for flight.

Religious objects had a disarming constancy. For years she'd been wanting to ditch the Ecstasy of Saint Teresa, but sacrilege was a risk. If only she'd been able to get rid of the tortured face in its brown madonna's hood when her father had left, or when she'd completed a degree at university, or met Matthew. Yet even now Saint Teresa struggled with the anguish of her bliss. There were no harps strumming for her, no smiles of resignation as God plucked on her nervous system like a zither.

She recalled her mother after her father had left, the mood of elation followed by the rather mechanical re-enactments of their life together. In the end there was sorrow at life's emptiness, at people's inability to accept this emptiness with humility. 'And when I think of him,' she'd said, 'down at Richmond dog meetings. You know how quick a dog race is. Ten seconds and it's over, with a young girl in a short skirt. It breaks my heart.'

Her mother had been brought up on fear, and perhaps it was fear which had left with her husband. Anyway, she'd lost that muscular faith which went with her youth, and a kind of flabby realism remained. 'I'm becoming stall fed,' she'd said, smiling. 'Go to Alice Springs if you've been asked there. You'll be better off.'

So Lucy had accepted Matthew's invitation to the desert. She felt she had little to lose, not even a mother's blessing. Yet she was uneasy about Matthew. At university he'd behaved in a disciplined, fastidious manner. If it hadn't been for his half-caste black skin people would have spoken against him. He'd organised the anti-Springbok demonstrations with offensive precision. The campus counter culture disapproved, found this medical student authoritarian in his dealings.

She remembered that game of football too well, the unruly crowd rewarded by the sight of a woman's blouse torn as on the covers of cheap paperbacks. Everywhere the noise of a fight, groups disappearing into quicksand, only to separate out again to see one more long hair dragged into a police wagon, complacently kneaded into the van by a housekeeper policeman, voice high and lady-like in his corset of muscle.

Cruel images came into her mind. In this country people had to control themselves. A match could light the world ablaze. And perhaps Matthew had realised, when all was said and done, how a university Hamlet could end up with more blood on the stage than the most determined Macbeth. He'd held himself back accordingly.

Perhaps in the desert there would be danger of

Europeans turning feral, stripping the country bare like cats, growing fat on the native species. Newcomers gained such a rapid ascendancy. She remembered how, in the old green country of the south-west, her grandfather had half admired the rabbits for their predominance.

Today he was probably buried with them, caught perhaps in one of those major tunnels that went for miles. When she was little, she recalled, he'd held a glass to the earth saying: 'Listen, Lucy, you can hear them in their hotel rooms, drinking and carousing. Imagine them, dear, with their pink eyes way into the night. Civilisation is being undermined by these herbivorous powder puffs and sometimes I think to myself "Good luck to 'em. The best of the British to 'em." '

The kindness of European gentlemen beckoned, tempting her into pity. How could she deny his good intentions. His patience had known no limits. He had learnt to live with the country, the unfaithful wife who slept with one conqueror after another. There was little heroism to be gained from such a situation.

Leaving Sydney had its dangers too. What if, like the fish avoiding the spear, she was unaware of the sun burning her level down. What was the use of leaving one danger and replacing it with another? Perhaps it was wrong to place her faith in the desert and that underground water Matthew had promised, the cold clear ice that came from as far away as New Guinea.

'There's hope for everyone in the Centre,' he'd said. 'Even for old Williemunga, one of my cousins.' He'd lost ninety per cent of his eyesight from trachoma. Matthew was probably operating on the old man now, the old man who had stayed alive in spite of day-long sleeping next to a petrol pump, drunk. He would consent to the operation because he was eager to see young women again.

There was hope in the future, even when memories followed the currents of her thoughts like birds. Nobody could say without hesitation that the birds were predatory. Perhaps they'd come to savour a sweet and shameless slipstream.

Wayne Thompson was married, and according to Adelaide, wizened like a jockey. Lucy shuddered. 'Don't go looking for trouble,' he'd warned years ago. 'You go looking for trouble like next door's tom.'

The fragility of the city came into her mind. What if someone were to pluck the wings off the Opera House as if it were a cicada. In the city playground she thought she could imagine such a thing. White cement wings plucked from a blue angel harbour. Nothing like the shame of a good plucking, or the city fallen, emptied out by the wind of its own emptiness. She imagined the shells of skyscrapers, their contents eaten out like oysters; clean office chimneys left to stand like fireplaces in old gold-mining towns.

She was glad to be leaving. 'You're going to Alice Springs,' her mother had said. 'I'm thinking of leaving Haberfield too. I've never liked it. It was your father's choice. Those Italian men now. I don't like them, sitting in shop windows and playing cards. I get upset for their women. They're in black before they're forty, and Gina's a good friend. She dresses her children beautifully. You should see the things she makes for them, two and three petticoats apiece. But her husband spends all his time paving their yard and flirting with younger women. That's not fair, is it? Then he comes home and sits in front of a good meal as if nothing has happened, and even Gina wants to get out. Even the Italians are getting out.'

There was indeed a different atmosphere in the suburb. Vicious ladies in straw hats had been replaced by strong cantankerous peasant women who liked children. The school too was changed. The Italians had put the nuns in their places. There was no fawning over the clergy now, no de Boscos in this new enlightenment.

'There was justice in the world,' laughed Lucy to herself. 'God took away the Latin Mass and gave them Italians to take its place. What plan could be diviner than that?'

In the distance there was always the strident green rectangle, the promise of luxury in the form of a lucerne paddock, where she and all the other animals could be set loose to graze. No longer nursery rhyme sheep on rollers, ludicrously stiff and upright amidst the farm technology, the world of men waiting sentinel at every orifice to spray, dip, drench for disease and profit.

More than ever before Lucy needed release. She would welcome the hellish temperature at the earth's centre. It would offer security. The nuns had barely withstood the Sydney weather. She placed them randomly in the main street of Alice Springs to see how long they could withstand the punishment. Instead, their black habits had so fiercely invited the heat, they were picked off immediately, and flown far away from the scorching earth.

Their ending was merciful. Christian. Not adult and sadistic like the ending of Peter Pan which she'd always abhorred. Peter, with all the benefits of being able to fly, had left poor old Hook, or was it Cook, to perish slowly inside a dark crocodile. This ancient reptile kept him prisoner. He was left to die like a convict to the sound of a clock ticking, hoping that of these long-lived animals, his would prove the exception. To die, hoping that the clock would stop ticking before he did, to allow him a little peace at the end. 'By Hook or by Cook,' whispered Lucy aloud. 'By Hook or by Cook I'll forgive the nuns, and save up my tears for when they are needed.'

The train had been stationary for over an hour. Her

mother had made a sending-off dress. It had bat sleeves to wave propitious breezes to her daughter.

Lucy felt she was destined for another island and there was a magic about heading off. The fullness of many hopes puffed out her sails.

Adelaide was there, chastened, relieved, polite to Mrs Stapleton. She shook out a spinnaker of handkerchief to cry into.

Thank God, thought Lucy, she'd chosen to go by train. A plane so glibly implied destination. Now she felt free, exposed, as she waited for the tide to take her out of Five Dock, Sydney, away from the low-tide bottles, tins of open tetanus, all the throat-cutting empty containers that lay the city waste and looking like the bottom of a dam.

At last they began to move. 'Goodbye,' called Lucy, looking back to the brolgas dancing their now tired farewells. As it gathered speed the train started threading houses together like beads on a rosary, threading suburban bungalows, red, detached and brutal, until they rattled like beads on an abacus.

One look backwards into the city's ugliness might bring bad luck. Perhaps she would be abandoned, left high and dry like Mrs Lot, turned into a 'pillow' (as it had been termed in the playground) of salt.

Seven hours out of Sydney Lucy looked out the window at the dry creek beds and green gullies winding across the south-west slopes. She liked the meandering relevance of a train, making a special detour to allow her to say goodbye. Soon they would be at Harden with its elegant railway station, dreary township. She'd gone there with her grandfather often enough. He had held the typical squatter's contempt for country towns, their meagre dependence on being a transport node, on having to supply food for the smaller holdings.

She wondered if Alice Springs would look the same. Would it have a long main street with that sense of dry whispering, an invitation to chatter between bushfires?

Harden was an extremely long thread of a place, like a tapeworm with rigor mortis, a parasite lured out from the sheep's intestine to grow thin and die. There were three hotels, a few shops, dogs and drunks.

Outside the new drive-in bottle shop was someone she recognised, a fat widow who used to chat with her grandfather. If the old man were alive, perhaps they would be talking together now, complaining of the grease left by shearers' hair on pillowslips, or the number of judges prejudiced against the black breed of collie at the last show. She thought she could imagine him, velour hat in hand, making little bowing gestures to discourage the flies, too polite to leave until he was dismissed.

In the distance she could see paddocks of Patterson's Curse showing a vivid penitential purple. Hadn't the farmers suffered enough without these beautiful weeds springing out of the earth like Salomes, leaving the sheep sick with desire, loading the bees heavy with pollen until they looked like dull and ungainly blowflies?

She loved this gentle, deceptive country, especially the huge igneous rocks the farmers had to plough around. Granite smooth, they were covered with a pale green lichen, the colour of grass after a light frost. Looking at these faded marbles, scattered indolently across the slopes to the world's edge, it really did seem to Lucy that the earth had properly cooled down. God had scattered his promises carelessly without needing the symmetry of a rainbow.

Lucy changed trains that night in Melbourne. She slept in her chrome and laminate sleeping compartment until she was woken up by sunlight spreading a keyboard through the venetians onto the opposite wall.

The country was so different now. Light, barren, dead animals as frequent as live. Cattle stations were beginning to appear. She remembered her grandfather's contempt for cows and cowhands. They were the newchums of the bush. They had brazen ways, spiteful animals that knocked down fences, eating the country down to a covering of brown suede. Cattle and America had formed a crude equation in his conversation. Even before he died, cowmen had been speaking of 'corrals' instead of mustering yards, wearing cowboy hats in preference to velour.

Sheep were England to him, the elegance of English properties with their fine homes and gentlemanly ways. He would have dressed his sheep in waistcoats had there been less wool on their backs. Of course it was snobbery, and she objected to it. Nevertheless he'd been very attached to his flock. He had always admired the way they ate their food so noiselessly, never fought over a patch of grass, and seemed to attach such little importance to their own persons that they could scarcely be deemed stupid.

She had two days in Adelaide before making her connection to Alice Springs. Taught at school to expect a free city, she'd always imagined Adelaide as the town where convicts had gone to escape, a city full of hacksaws and files hidden under park benches.

For the first time in her life she was seeing a planned city. This was as far as authority had gone. Yet she could feel authority everywhere, in the tree-lined avenues, the rows of bluestone houses parcelled into the valleys and foothills of distant ranges. There were no sea breezes. None of the windswept energy which characterised the east, or those cities where people had been compelled to stay.

She thought of the splayed hand of Sydney's distrusting suburbs, sprawling over and flattening headlands, sinking into gullies and swamps. It was a city weighed down by human waste, now cheekily offering itself to newcomers. The cathedral she'd been confirmed in had been built on a municipal dump. It was in the centre of the city. Nowadays no one would guess at irregularity in its dullness, in the murky brown redundancy of its buttresses.

An insecure city had to be weighed down so it wouldn't blow away. There were no neat grid lines which could hold Sydney down. Its shallowness was protected by torpidity, like the creeks heavy with mud which crossed the rest of the country. Security lay in a lack of visibility, in a winding mud scrape which posed as a river to taunt the thirsty.

She was thirsty, her spirit dry in a country neglected by words, hopes, dreams, where all kinds of diabolical bargains could be forged because nothing was written down, forged and re-forged like sand dunes shifting to accommodate wind direction. She remembered her pen and ink scrawl which had so infuriated Mother de Bosco. The nun had indeed been entitled to something better. To a generous ripple of blue across the page.

She felt sad, thinking of the story of Saint Bernadette clawing at the soil in France. It had filled her with pity so many years ago. She'd not been supposed to feel that way. The dry sandstone stump of Sydney gothic rose reproachfully into her thoughts. The stumbling block, where intellectuals attending the university were beheaded. There it was in her mind now, pushing out of its patched colonial coat to interrupt her thoughts. It was one of the ugliest buildings in a city which had little respect for learning.

There were few countries in the world so neglected by written history as hers. Yet it was useless to desire an illicit past. That was the sign of the adolescent. At twenty-two she was determined to show her maturity.

The train left Adelaide for Maree where there was a change to a narrow-gauge track. Even the arteries of a railway, thought Lucy, could diminish.

She hadn't spoken to anybody for over four days. This was a novelty, and there were at least two more privileged days left. It was so much easier to say one's goodbyes in private. Saying goodbye was like going to confession. She knew she would be forgiven for specific actions, but she needed time to ponder the general state of her credibility.

The train had been built during the twenties. In terms of fixtures and accoutrements, it showed an effortless elitism in favour of first-class passengers, like herself. If people travelled first class at least once in their lives, she believed they would see that there was a certain amount of discipline involved in wasting money. But she had to be careful. She was thinking like her father.

Lucy's compartment was wood-panelled, with heavily worked iron fixtures capable of dropping down, pulling out, extending, it seemed, well beyond the life of the train, and possibly the town to which they were heading.

There were several redundant carriages, one with a piano, the others with lounges. Everyone took for granted the destination of fellow traveller. Thus the atmosphere was one of a committee of investigation obliged to find the reasons and motives for an established outcome. People became curious about each other; what they would say to explain themselves.

Passengers strode through the carriages like proud animals about to be exhibited. One of the cars had already been given over to a game of cards. There was much enthusiasm for that circle, with its fringe of shy grandmothers.

Lucy had put herself down for 'first meal sittings' upon the advice of the steward.

'Tablecloth's cleaner, more choice on the menu. I usually recommend the first. Why not? Reckon the train's so blooming slow, why not get in for your chop early, before you get too restless.'

He wore a white waistcoat with a stretch of gold chain to pull it wide across his middle, and black trousers. His face was red, a butcher's face too long in the freezer room.

The air-conditioning was very effective, with a burning quality reminiscent of dry ice. Lucy, in a light cardigan, found it difficult to imagine the temperature outside.

The trees had begun to look spindly. Their leaves were like hypodermics. She imagined them injecting fire into her blood, and in the distance spiking the blue flat underside of the sky like grass tickling a lizard's belly.

It would soon be lunch. No doubt she would be seated with other weak-minded people who had chosen to take advice.

'He told me around midday,' said the older man seated at her table. 'I like his idea of around.'

'I suppose,' said Lucy, 'seeing as though the train prides itself on being late, it takes just as equal and perverse a pride in serving its meals early.'

They looked at her with total blankness, as if she had described a death in her family.

'Late,' the younger man repeated, clutching at a word he understood. 'It was three months late during the floods.'

He was no more than twenty, looking forward to his next promotion with a permanent effort of concentration on his face.

'The train doesn't run to schedules,' said the older man's wife. 'However, I am determined to have a good time. Regardless.'

'But we never eat before twelve,' said her husband.

'In and around,' she contradicted, using her prepositions with the heaviness of railway cutlery. 'Anyway I'm Jan,' she said to Lucy, 'and this is my husband Lionel. I believe you're Jason,' she said to the younger man. 'Jason's come up to see his girlfriend.'

Lucy looked at them, disbelieving a destination in common. She sat with the intention not to talk, to eat her meal as quickly and quietly as possible.

'And what are you to the Alice?' asked Lionel, with the impertinence of a paying guest.

'I'm going to teach at the college,' said Lucy. 'Turkey.'

The waiter wrote the number of her table.

'Who's having the lamb then?' asked the waiter. 'Okay. One lamb, three turkeys.'

'One lamb, three turkeys,' repeated Lionel familiarly, 'and a waiter in a monkey suit.'

There was an attempt to laugh.

'Don't be gauche,' said his wife, looking apologetically to Lucy. 'We're going to see our son.' She said this as if in explanation for her husband's rudeness. 'He works on a station. It's a rough and ready life. Rough and ready.'

The train travelled at fifteen miles per hour, making a lot of noise, as if preparing to stop at some mirage in the flatness.

It was an extraordinary invasion of privacy to sit at a table with strangers and eat with them. Lucy thought, for the first time, that she could feel the smallness, the indecency of life in a small town.

'And where are you from, dear?' asked Jan. 'Oh really. We have friends in Sydney. They are lovely people. Although their daughter does go to school in Melbourne.'

'I come from Adelaide,' said Jason, dividing his turkey

into neat pieces of string. 'It's not a bad meal, is it? Five courses. I'm thinking of buying some land at Flagstaff Hill.'

'We have some fine restaurants in Melbourne,' said Jan, 'but I'm content to eat anything at the moment, provided I'm not the chef. When I'm not cooking it's a real holiday.'

'I'll say,' said her husband.

The people at the table were, with swashbuckling confidence, razing the meal to the ground. It made Lucy nervous to think about the future, the kind of licence she would have to allow people.

'Shall I get the water jug from the other table?' asked Jan.

'Wouldn't do that,' said her husband, bluntly. 'I wouldn't trust the water on these long trips. They've had to store it somewhere, you know, in rusty old vats and lead pipes.'

The ground outside was looking stony and mutilated, steam rising from a canvas of cracked earth. Lucy did not want to turn her mind to the triviality of life in a compartment, a small community in the middle of nowhere. How would she be able to avoid such people, their idiotic prejudices, their pre-fab pasts? She wanted a future. When she looked outside to the country she almost believed she could have it.

'Look at that,' said Lionel. 'Two emus. I've never seen them out of a zoo before.'

'Maybe it's one of those new-style game parks,' said his wife, 'like they have in Africa.'

'No.' Lionel scraped some mustard relish across his lamb. 'Definitely not.'

'But there's a captive audience here on the train,' said Jan, who rather liked the idea of being captured, who had explored, endlessly, the possibilities of being abducted.

'Captive,' laughed Lionel, 'but not paying.'

'When I was little I was given an emu egg,' said Jan sentimentally. 'It was smaller and more fragile than one would have expected.'

'Like yourself,' said Lionel rudely, 'when I married you.'

The ground was torn, vandalised. Lucy observed the mutilation creating updraughts of heat, spiralling from the very heart of the earth, forcing their way through cracks and crevices to wind upwards into the sky. Bushes span inside these cones of air, 'thermals', as Jason called them.

A period of silence followed. Even Jan and Lionel stopped talking to watch the thermals twisting the dead puppet branches of trees, bushes, tumbleweed, making them dance, skip and spin across the red plains and into the sky. Lucy sank into her seat. The side to side shunting of the train made her sea-sick. Outside the spirals added to her dizziness. The desert was not flat as she'd expected.

That night she suffered from indigestion and an inability to sleep. The narrow gauge caused a roughness in the ride. The train seemed more like a ghost train where the interest lay in darkness, in sudden vaulting changes of direction. Perhaps there were spirals underneath the train, an army of ghosts lifting it ever so slightly off its tracks.

In such open country, phantoms were no threat. They were merely infinity lost in infinity. In the moonlight the country looked blue, with a trusting softness. She felt that it was no more frightening than a small lost child. There was none of the tangled, secret undergrowth found on the coast.

When they reached Oodnadatta, Lucy nearly fell out of bed with the surprise. It was a strange town with a high tin fence to keep out. What? Like a town out of the Arabian Nights, it drew its cogent slash of steel across sand. Corrugated iron rippled in the bright light, as did the steely surface of sand dunes, the barbed surface, held together by spinifex.

The town had come to look at the train. People were there to collect mail and provisions. Some were selling opals, boomerangs and honey from the local trees. After several hundred miles, it was an oasis, a series of quick transactions through train windows, more rapid and joyous than anything observed in Rundle Mall.

A number of townspeople looked eagerly into the train's compartments. Perhaps they were hoping for people undressing. Buttock against window. A shelf of breast. A swing of sweet flesh before the close of shutters.

Lionel was chatting to a young aboriginal girl. She did not look at his face, but merely watched the movements of his hands.

Jason and Jan had struck up a friendship. They were spending a lot of time talking about commitment, the problem Jason was having with women expecting too much. As they walked together, Jan's studied amiability, her open sandals and painted toes, provided the necessary complement to the young boy's incompleteness. Lucy felt like laughing. Matthew looked so different from this healthy young t-bone.

Twice a week the train called at Oodnadatta to engage in honest trade. There seemed to Lucy nothing more intriguing in human nature than the desire to have something owned by someone else, even when it had no bearing on survival. This strange acquisitiveness had its material and non-material aspects. If it were truly honest, it involved a sacrifice on the part of the seller as well as the buyer. Commercialism was ugly when it lacked reciprocity and balance. There had to be some sort of emotional commitment to everything. Carried to its logical extreme, the ideal sale was one where the two parties fell in love.

The train started up. The townspeople waved it laden into the sky. So many of its passengers, went the Oodnadatta wisdom, had no idea of life in the bush, with their city stilettos, binoculars, nylon tights, socks and sandals. Thank God they'd met real bush people, at least bought what would remain appropriate, memorable. There was no stone in the world as unturned as the opal. A Coober Pedy opal, full of reproachful fire, or a boomerang from the district, heavy, lopsided and powdered with ochre. At least now, as opinion went, the people on the train had experienced something worthwhile, were protected by sacred objects and would complete their journey safely. Only the aboriginal girl was dissatisfied. She would not come to the station again, not until she was older.

The closer the train got to Alice Springs, the redder the soil became. Ghost gums, in their whiteness, pushed up and out of this blood colour like severed arteries. Their leaves were a dainty adolescent growth, a curious false beard of green.

It was odd how such undisciplined, untouched country should appear contrived. The mountain ranges were like ancient stage scenery, steep, stony, eroded, placed in overlapping rows like stage wings.

The vegetation appeared painted and pasted on, as if the gold-pink bark of trees had stopped breathing under a coat of white stage make-up. It pretended to be a slow production, with a tired, loyal cast. What did she care? It was her first time in this particular theatre and she was ready to applaud. She was ready and waiting for the dramatic slash in the mountain ranges which opened up the town of Alice Springs.

6

The railway station was in the centre of town. It was a fifties construction with a pink and blue interior. A smell of plastic verdure emanated from the walls, and there was a curiously neat row of flies, dead on their backs, under the information counter.

The heat was intense. She hadn't been prepared for its strength. She felt punch-drunk, weightless. The feeling of weightlessness was already causing a certain extravagance within her, inviting her to jump, crater to crater, amongst the dry hills surrounding the town.

'Lucy. Why aren't you waiting inside?' Matthew had waited two hours for the train. It was late.

'I'm sorry,' she said, pleased with his dark looks, pale clothing. 'It was a fascinating trip up.'

Jan and Lionel jostled by, darting an arrow of disapproval at them. Jason walked behind, looking embarrassed.

'Do you know them?' asked Matthew, not waiting for an answer. 'You'll have to pick up your luggage tomorrow. I'm afraid it comes separately. You must stay with me for a while. I'd like you to stay.'

'We'll see,' said Lucy. 'Thank you very much anyway.'

'I was so pleased you wrote to me,' said Matthew. 'I showed your letter to everyone, to my mother, Titus, Marjorie, and even a priest.'

'I've forgotten what I told you in the letter,' said Lucy, looking down the wide, shaded main street of the town. 'What's the temperature?'

'Forty-four degrees,' replied Matthew.

'That's terrible,' said Lucy, looking with disbelief at the steam rising from sun-soft bitumen.

'I can show you around if you'd like,' said Matthew rather formally, inviting Lucy into his four-wheel drive.

'I'd love to see it,' said Lucy. 'I didn't expect so many hills around the town. They look two-dimensional in the sun.'

'Some people find them claustrophobic,' said Matthew, afraid to touch her, to feel the distance which had already come between them.

'Nonsense,' she denied. 'They look old and frail. Like you could just push them over if you wanted to get out. Are all the houses the same?' She thought she could smell camel.

'Some of them have nice gardens,' said Matthew, pointing to a dull-mauve brick house with an ostentatious sprinkler system. Between the bougainvillea and the ornamental wattle tree was a huge trail bike looking like a greedy bee with swollen abdomen.

'The gardens are very green,' agreed Lucy, secretly surprised by the town's uniformity. To her, neither men nor towns looked better in uniform.

'You don't have to find excuses,' said Matthew. 'I won't be offended. My brother hates it here. He only stays in town to look after my mother.'

'I'm sorry,' said Lucy apologetically, looking at the double-brick bungalows, their small windows designed to keep out the heat. 'Why did you show my letter to a priest?'

'He's a friend of my brother.'

'That's not a reason. I'm dying for a drink.'

'We can go to my house,' said Matthew, 'on the Eastside where there are trees. There's a fantastic hill behind too. Red boulders polished smooth. Titus laughs at the dreamtime droppings. The kangaroo was a lot bigger once.'

'I'm looking forward to meeting your family,' she said.

'My mother lives down the street. Titus and I share a house.'

'Where's your father?'

'He left a long time ago. He was white.'

'Do you remember him?'

'Not much. My mother speaks well of him. He was a painter like my brother, not very good from what he left in the house, but perhaps he took his best away with him.'

'Does your mother live alone?'

'Not really. Our cousins live next door to her, and there are lots of them. I don't like them much. They're drunks except for Henry.'

They crossed the causeway, the strip of fraying bitumen across the river bed to the Eastside. Along the banks of the Todd were sheets of cast iron, aboriginal shelters, and in the sandy bed itself were the grey patches of campfire extinguished.

'What do you call these trees?'

'River reds.'

They were ageing aristocrats of eucalypts, twists of noble grey rising from the sand, streaked with light. A blessed and indifferent commune in the small square of town.

They pulled up to an old fibro house with a wooden verandah. The paint was pale green and peeling in the heat. Close behind was the dramatic red-orange hill of stones. Some were small and delicate. Others, large, red, almost threatened to roll down on to the house. Spinifex closed up spaces in the hill but seemed to add little to a sense of stability. In the front of the house there was an old walnut tree, the only one in town. It gave shade and cast black lace on to the iron roof.

'This is lovely,' said Lucy into the empty well of Matthew's disbelief. 'No, I mean it. This is everything I was hoping for from Alice Springs.'

'Really?' he said. 'I thought you'd like the other parts of town better. Most people seem to.'

Lucy was disappointed that he hadn't anticipated her feelings better.

'It's perfect.' She continued on into the interior of the house with its large rooms, the wood stove in the kitchen. 'Perfect.'

Titus came out from one of the bedrooms to meet Lucy.

'If this is all that you were hoping for, then you can go back tomorrow with a clear conscience.' Matthew blushed, and Titus, seeing his brother's embarrassment, apologised.

'I'm sorry. Of course we expect you to stay longer than that. I'll see you later. I've got things to do.'

He disappeared quickly, out the front door.

'I'm sorry,' said Matthew. 'He's not usually rude, even to whites.'

'It doesn't matter,' said Lucy. 'I'll only be staying overnight.'

'You must stay longer than that,' said Matthew significantly. 'Later you can meet my mother.'

'I'd like to,' said Lucy, wondering why she'd come all this way to establish how little they had in common.

Mrs Hayes was a full blood of the Aranda tribe. A large woman with clear eyes and legs like fire sticks. When she put a tablecloth on the old wooden table, she seemed to stroke it smooth so many more times than was necessary.

'Lucy,' she said, 'Matthew has told me so much about you. Pleased to meet you.' She touched Lucy's shoulders and looked at her. 'You must excuse my bruise,' she said, pointing to a shiny patch of purple on her cheek. 'I had to give Henry a hiding. He's getting too sure of himself, telling everyone not to drink then chasing me when I get drunk, taking advantage of me if you see what I mean. He knows I'll come round so why does he have to wait till I get drunk. He's a hypocrite. I've warned him often enough. He's turning into a real big feller, and he'll get a few hidings for it. Anyway Lucy you'll excuse this family, like Matthew does. He's a gifted boy with his doctor's knife. I'm proud of him, like I was of his father. You can see a picture of my husband with his painting knife on the wall. Sam was a rascal, my husband you know was a rascal. No responsibility, but we had plenty of good times. Black or white, people need a hiding. They need a good hiding, and to keep a clean arse. Do you understand, dear? You don't take too much notice of people, do you?'

'I don't know,' she hesitated, 'but I think my father deserved a good hiding.'

Mrs Hayes looked pleased.

'I've made some tea. Tell me about your father.'

'There isn't much,' said Lucy. 'He left my mother. He gambled their money.'

'And what did your mother do to him?'

'Nothing,' said Lucy. 'She used to complain.'

Mrs Hayes looked surprised for a few moments, but quickly resumed her composure.

'Then she must have done a lot of complaining. She must have got into his dreams somehow. Otherwise he wouldn't have had to leave. She must have been a powerful and determined woman your mother, a powerful woman.'

Lucy accepted the transference gratefully. Mrs Hayes poured the tea and smiled at her.

'Have you met my other son? He's as secretive as a snake with its belly empty. The snake is our totem. The rainbow snake. Handsome and dangerous. When they initiated him, Jimbajimbi wanted to do the extra things they do for a sorcerer. But he was outvoted. Titus is a half-caste. So Matthew became the doctor, and everyone tells me now that they are glad.'

It was very confusing for Lucy, the way Mrs Hayes slalomed so recklessly between two cultures, the way she rose out of it all, without being told what she had lost, nor what she was to gain. In the desert, it seemed, time was so vast and unimpressive it outstared culture, outstared itself.

Lucy felt a strong liking for the woman already. She had come expecting to feel sorry for her, to find her degraded by white civilisation. Instead Mrs Hayes was taking everything in the portion it was offered. She would not go hungry in any sense. There were things Lucy wanted to learn from her, good and bad. The time of comfortable silence was ending. Matthew finished his tea quickly.

'She really is a good woman.' he said after they'd left. 'I know she gets drunk, and fights, but it's not very often.'

'You don't have to apologise,' said Lucy. 'I like her.'

She walked back to the house. Heat and flies were blurring her senses together into a hum of heat, a vibrating whirr of desert machinery. It was difficult to hear what Matthew was saying. There were many impressions jumping about in her mind, and like cattle tics, they could be hard to get rid of.

'I think your mother is great,' she said, adjusting to the coolness of Matthew's house. 'Why did your father leave? Do you hear from him?'

'We've had two letters,' he said. 'The same number that you've written to me. He's living in Indonesia, running a fruit stall and painting when he has the time. The letters didn't tell us much. He sent some Indonesian currency which my mother hasn't bothered to change over.'

'Would she like to go to Indonesia?' asked Lucy, worried by Matthew's inference.

'I think she'd be happy to see the coast of Australia. I'm taking her there at the end of the year.'

Titus came out quickly from the kitchen.

'No you're not,' he said. 'It won't mean anything to her at her age. She won't want to leave the country, where her spirit is safe. She's not a fool.'

'How old is she?' asked Lucy, though the question immediately struck her as irrelevant.

'She was old ten years ago,' said Titus proudly. 'She has a lot of authority, and the old men come to her for advice. Not only that, she has a lot more freedom as to whom she sleeps with. Don't you think,' he said looking at Matthew, 'she's getting sick of Henry? She should have given him away when he began selling those dingo pups and shell postcards to the tourists. He's become so unctuous lately.'

'How much authority has she got?' asked Lucy, intrigued. Her mother had none whatsoever.

'Well obviously authority depends on the person,' said Titus. 'But she had worked with the kadaitcha man on one or two occasions. She had Valerie killed, the woman who tried to poison her husband's drinking water. She could probably get a number of people killed, if she wanted, without the kadaitcha man. But she uses the law.'

'The elders have consulted with her before forming a council,' said Matthew. 'She has a reputation for giving good advice. Her authority was even stronger before she took up with my father.'

'I don't think that weakened her authority,' said Titus, annoyed. He left the room without further comment.

Matthew and Lucy talked until dark. Both of them were relieved he had left. Lucy had lots of questions she wanted to ask, mundane problems that would have made Titus scornful and uneasy.

'I'll have to find you a chair,' said Mr Robbins. 'I have put in requisition after requisition for more chairs. But down in Canberra they think we sit on bourree logs. Perhaps I could bring you a stool from the music room. Would that be all right?'

'Of course,' said Lucy to the principal, wondering where on earth they sat the students.

'I know you won't be starting at the college for a month Mrs Stapleton.'

'Two weeks,' she interrupted, politely. 'I'm not married.'

'Exactly,' he said. He was a small man, sitting in his office with his grandson, looking like some fond antique unicorn out of a children's storybook. 'So it won't hurt to finalise things now. You came up by train I gather.'

His grandson, a retarded youth, sat nearby with a plate of cream biscuits in front of him.

'I love the Ghan,' he said. 'It's called after the Afghans, you know. There were a lot of them in town once. "Mobs" of them, as the locals say.'

'How exciting,' said Lucy, looking at the soggy biscuits and hoping she would not be offered one.

'Yes,' he said enthusiastically, 'this town would have looked like a set for Lawrence of Arabia, once. Have you seen the film? Peter O'Toole is one of my favourite actors. Even Damian enjoyed it, didn't you Damian?'

The young boy couldn't answer; there was too much biscuit packed into his mouth.

'He takes such a long time to chew his food,' said Mr Robbins, 'and the only things he'll eat are biscuits. So that's why we keep them in front of him as much as possible.'

'Is he your son?' asked Lucy.

This pleased Mr Robbins. 'Grandson,' he said. 'My daughter teaches at the high school.'

'Would you like to see proof of my qualifications?' asked Lucy. It was a strange sort of interview, like looking up an uncle in a foreign country. There was no formality, only a pleasant sense of obligation.

'Of course,' he said, 'if we can get more people like yourself we might be able to convince the government about starting a university. I've been working on them for years. The problem is, as you know, we are not an independent territory yet. Our legislature is confined to certain areas, and of course the money comes from Canberra.'

'But the Commonwealth Government can be generous?'

'With money,' he said, 'not people. All these bally staff ceilings. I've had it up to here, up to the ceiling if you like. We were lucky to get approval for you.'

'I'm glad you did,' said Lucy.

'So am I,' he said. 'Of course our lack of independence has its good points; car registration is cheap, it's easy to get a liquor licence. Not that I drink much nowadays. Damian keeps me on my toes. He hasn't got his own toes you know.'

Lucy wanted to smile politely, but it would have to be a laugh or nothing at all. She just couldn't smile.

Mr Robbins continued with heroic vagueness. 'There's an acute housing shortage here. I don't know how long it will take us to get you a house. I've been waiting for mine for over two years.'

'Where do you live?' asked Lucy, surprised.

'In the caravan you see parked outside.'

'But that must be terrible.'

'It's hot, of course,' he said, 'but there's an air-conditioner.'

'Two years,' repeated Lucy.

'Don't feel sorry for us,' he said, unconsciously including Damian. 'I'm a gypsy at heart. I've always been a gypsy. You see I can't get a house because I'm classified as prestige personnel. I won't get any rental subsidy unless I move into a prestige home. But they get snapped up quickly by senior police and judges. But I think there might be one fairly soon.'

'How many people are there in the General Studies Department?' asked Lucy. The specificity of her question seemed to encourage further digression. Age could be perverse.

'The last person to get a prestige house was a magistrate. He sent me round some cumquat brandy to make up for it. A nice man really, but I think he'd over-sugared the brandy. You should get about fifteen students on the first night, and with any luck you'll keep them. There'll be some aborigines in your group probably. What a noble race. I just wish the people in the town could be a little more tolerant.'

Mr Robbins caught his grandson putting his fist firmly into the corner of a chair. He jumped out from behind his desk and slapped the boy's fist until it opened out, full of biscuit.

'He puts them into the chair linings,' he said, 'and the cleaners complain. Thank heavens I don't have to supervise the teachers; that would be too much altogether. Sit down and behave yourself. I allow a good deal of lassitude in designing courses. Basically you can teach them what you want. Nothing too highbrow of course. I wouldn't bother with Kingsley Amis.'

'No,' said Lucy, 'nor would I.'

'Who do you enjoy then, dear?'

'Nabokov, Gorky, Austen, Eliot, Melville, Balzac . . .'

'Not P. G. Wodehouse?'

'I think I'll have to ask the students what they would like.'

'That's a fresh approach,' he said. 'You're such a fresh young thing. You can't imagine how we need people like you.' He shook her hand until it felt stale and limp. 'Come and see me if you have any problems. They don't have to relate to the college you know. Come round for a chat and we can make up a file. Would you like that?'

Lucy left. She would explore the corridor of shade down into the shopping centre. There were two rows of large native cedars, leafy and covered with smooth summer seed pods.

As she passed through the cool leaf tunnel, she noticed crosses on the trees. They were painted like red swastikas on the corrugated bark. Lucy wondered what these red emblems stood for. She thought of the Passover. Perhaps each of these wonderful trees was going to be spared. The town's vandals were proving themselves redoubtable.

At school, crosses had been etched on the backs of desks to identify those with dandruff. Suzie and Mavis had once drawn a moulting cross on the back of her desk. It had been red, with a spray of white Derwent down to the floor.

There was no doubt about it, it was odd to see blood incisions on trees. Perhaps the aborigines had made them as an adjunct to initiation ceremonies. Sister Nagle would have approved, possibly improved. What a phenomenon for a small modern town to have such emblems. She would have to find out more about them.

A group of men walked past, legs tourniqued by white long socks, feet laced tightly into hush puppies. Any darker their freckles would be melanoma. A Seurat-like frieze of dots, they made in the sun a dizzy, drunken dance of freckles.

Souvenir shops, pubs, tourist arcades all in a perfect grid. The men had been talking alcoholically about Canberra. A group of aborigines passed, wearing cowboy hats in the white heat of midday, cutting down the sun's reflection, maximising the dark surfaces of their faces. Limping beside them at great speeds were dogs with sawn-off muzzles. Lucy felt frightened. Earlier that morning she'd seen one of the men in the river bed, threatening his friend with a flagon.

She went into a cafe and sat by the window to drink her coffee. It was only natural to feel foolish and helpless when one encountered for the first time a group so indigenous to the country. They were probably the most indigenous people in the world. Hitler might have envied their purity had they laid claim to it, had he not been colour blind.

She watched a drunken aborigine nursing his dog, whispering into its one blue heeler ear, stroking its dingo torso. The man crossed the road with the dog in his arms. 'Be careful,' he seemed to be saying to it, with an affectionate whisper into its muzzle. When they reached the other side of the road he gave the dog a firm kick in the arse and sent it away.

He was joined by another group, the women built like tropical houses, mammaries on stilts, using their size to advantage, whipping up a cyclone of dust, anger and sheer brute bullying around the men as they walked.

The men looked smaller but no more intimidated by size than the cattle dog in a herd of stubborn Angus.

'How was your coffee?' asked the waiter.

'Fine,' replied Lucy, picking out some stones of melted bitumen from her shoes.

'You're getting an eyeful of coon this morning, aren't you?' he said looking out of the window. 'It's not so bad when you get used to them.'

'It's not so bad now,' said Lucy, surprised by the rather shoe-shine nature of his prejudice.

'You'd think different if you had to live here.'

'I am going to live here,' she said. 'I've got a job at the college.'

'I thought as much,' he said. 'You don't look like a tourist. You'll be teaching my wife then. They said they were bringing someone up from the south to teach my wife. I told her that she had to get out of the house, and find herself an interest. Women should have interests these days, don't you think?'

'Stands to reason.' said Lucy, ignoring the sexual emphasis he had placed on 'interests'.

'Can I have another coffee?' she said. She definitely didn't like this man with his presumptuous, low-slung trousers, his see-through shirt and his enlarged adam's apple. Stupid really, she should have left. Ugliness was creating an inertia within her.

'They all start off like you,' he said. He had been preparing his case as he made the froth for her cappuccino. 'Do-gooders from the south thinking they have the answers. What do you think about my wife being chased across the causeway last month? A whole pack of them out for a good time.'

'I suppose there were about ten of them?' asked Lucy, thinking of childhood verse.

'At least,' he said. 'They came up from the river bed, smelling like camels on heat.'

'Did they manage to catch your wife?' she asked.

'No,' he replied, almost ashamed.

'Then she must be a pretty fast lady. I'll look forward to having her in my English class.'

He left quickly, shrunken and flaccid.

She tried to feel compassion for the littleness of the man's spirit. It was right for him to feel vulnerable, on the edge of existence. Perhaps the heat had got inside his head, like a bellows, puffing out failure with thoughts of hate and revenge.

Lucy went outside once more. Under the shade of the cedar, she breathed in the distance which separated her from Sydney. It was a powerful distance. It grew out of the heat as if it were preparing her for some absurd and remote contest she felt she had little chance of winning.

Muscle-bound and inactive, she felt she had little chance of winning.

'What's the meaning of those red crosses you see on all the cedar trees?' she asked Matthew.

'They're going to cut them down,' he said, quickly, wondering if she was ever going to drop her doggedly friendly manner towards him.

'Why?'

'The ones with markings on them have been found diseased.'

'They look all right to me.'

'Most of them got diseased after the last council meeting,' said Matthew, smiling.

'But they're such beautiful trees,' said Lucy. 'They're the most beautiful things in the town.'

She fell silent. There was no answer to the slash and burn techniques of Europeans living precarious lives here in the Centre. No cherry-blossom kits to decipher the eternal mysteries of the seasons; merely heat and lack of it, shade and lack of shade. Life had the two-dimensional flatness of vaudeville, the false bonhomie of a people dispossessed.

'The trees are a symptom,' said Matthew. 'The whites feel threatened because of land rights.'

'How much land have you asked for?'

'One-third,' said Matthew.

'We won't get that much,' said Titus, interrupting. He had overheard most of their conversation. 'We'll be lucky to get twenty per cent, and it won't be the good country either.'

'It'll be crown land, won't it?' asked Lucy.

'For the most part,' said Titus, 'which is why we'll get it. Nobody wants it.'

'But there must be some controversial cases,' said Lucy.

'Some of them are made controversial,' said Titus, with emphasis. 'When a claim was made a few miles out of town, on traditional land, a group of whites loaded the whole settlement on the backs of their trucks to disprove traditional ownership. They loaded all the corrugated iron, canvas, utensils, weapons and took them to another site. They were hoping to fool the court.'

'What I can't understand,' said Lucy, 'is why they leased part of Arnhem Land back to the Australian Government.'

'Kakadu National Park, you're talking about? They're too reasonable,' said Titus angrily. 'Reason is the weapon of the status quo. Minorities, by definition, have to be unreasonable.'

'I'm more optimistic than Titus,' said Matthew, looking intently at Lucy. There was still some hope she cared for him. 'I suppose it's the illusion of being able to heal.'

'Let's sit out on the verandah,' said Titus. But neither Lucy nor Matthew wanted to leave the table. He left them and stood in the doorway full stretch. A wire and slouch cliché of the stockman, his profile caught the afternoon sun. The impression left as he made a quick shy movement out the door.

'I think Titus is making an effort to be friendly,' he said to Lucy, 'probably for my sake.'

7

On her first night at college, Lucy caught the caretaker urinating on the lawn.

'Don't tell me,' he said. 'There can't be a class tonight. The last I heard the approval hadn't come through from Canberra.'

He took off at great speed to the principal's caravan, his khaki shorts clapping together in the manner of gauchos.

'Just as I thought,' he said, loudly enough for Lucy to hear. He wanted to regain control of the situation, a posture forced upon him by having pissed on the college grounds and not a private stretch of grass.

'Then how'll she get paid?'

Lucy could see the pixie face of Robbins through the window of his iron-lung living space.

'Has she filled in the 29B yet?' asked the caretaker. 'Then can I have the key to the office?'

'Do you think I'll get paid?' asked Lucy, cautiously.

'Which room will I put her in?' he shouted to the small face in the caravan. 'No. Too many typewriters. She'll have to go in Room 4. Could you ring stores and ask them to have the air-conditioner fixed tomorrow?'

Mr Robbins waved to Lucy and disappeared. The caretaker then put on the grumbling demeanour that people with an armoury of keys feel obliged to assume.

'They can wait,' he said, as they walked past a number of Lucy's students. 'You'll have to fill out the forms.'

The night was extremely hot. It was natural class

99

should start with a long delay. No doubt the students would be dissatisfied, but what could she do? Bureaucracy had intervened.

When she arrived in the shabby room the lights had been on for twenty minutes. Huge numbers of moths were already bombarding the neon-white melting tubes over her head. Her students were muttering amongst themselves and grumbling.

A fan went slowly over their heads, as if to count the paltry number of students present, to save her taking a roll. If one of them were to stand up perhaps the fan would take off his or her head. Oranges and Lemons say the bells of chipper, chopper, chipper, chopper last man's head head off.

The corpses of flies had begun to collect at the bases of chairs. Insects flew everywhere in the bright light. Already many of the students were killing, swiping, and leaving little blood trails on their legs.

'I'm sorry,' said Lucy. 'We haven't got an air-conditioner yet. We must begin to talk of literature. Could you bring insect repellent with you tomorrow?'

'I've got some mosquito coils at home,' said a big man. 'I'll bring them in.'

Lucy stood in front of the blackboard, where their eyes had directed her to stand. It was covered with chalk, a grey-white surface of moon dust. Moon dust whispered Lucy to herself. She was in a different world, and it was the surface of this blackboard which justified her existence, a vast expenditure to the people below.

'The first thing I want to discuss with you is your reading preferences. Perhaps we can study a novel, or a poem that you are interested in. I don't care if it's P. G. Wodehouse or Hemingway or Montserrat. Anybody.'

Whether or not Lucy was waiting for applause, she was soon to see that there was no reaction whatever to her proposal.

'Do you read books?' she asked, expecting them to laugh, to offer her Peter Benchley's latest, or even Morris West. But there was silence. 'Have you ever read a book?' she asked. 'Is there anyone in this class who has ever read a book?'

'I didn't come here for books,' said one of the men. 'I come to improve me spelling, so I can fill out requisition forms and things like that. You can't get anywhere without being able to do them. I'm as good as the next joker, except when it comes to finishing touches. And those forms, if I could do them I might get a promotion.'

His head sank back into his neck after the effort of talking. He looked determined now to rest on his laurels, on the globe of flesh that supported his world.

'I've begun reading George Johnston,' said a small thin eager woman. '*My Brother Jack*. I've got a brother called Jack, and when I saw that book in Sydney last trip down I thought it would give him a kick to see it. My husband, I think you've met him, he thinks I should finish it because it's good to have interests in life, but I'm not really enjoying it. Have you read it?'

'Yes, ' said Lucy, 'but we want a book that you find accessible.'

'I'm not too proud to want a spelling bee,' said another man in the corner.

'That's right,' said another.

'Well I'm sorry, but I disagree. I'm Mrs White from the Shell Garage in Todd Street and this course has been billed as a literature course. Spelling is not the reason I've come. You see I enrolled in music last year, and the same thing happened. They told me that there were these new expensive practice pianos brought up from the south and I was thrilled. I've had some training in the piano, you know, and I can read music. I cooked a week's worth of casseroles and put them in the fridge so I could come to the evening classes. The keyboards didn't have the necessary number of octaves. I couldn't play any classical music. I had to give up the idea of Beethoven, and play with ruddy earphones on.

'When I heard they were bringing up a trained teacher from the south with a good background in English, I couldn't believe my luck, and now they tell me they want spelling or whatever it is. This hasn't been billed as a spelling course. If people can't read or write then they have to make their own arrangements. The government is running a course for the aborigines in spelling, and I don't see why some of these men can't go along.'

The atmosphere had become provocative. Lucy felt more like a bad puppeteer than a teacher as she attempted to settle various demands in one stale plot.

'There's no reason why we can't have spelling and literature,' she said to her audience, 'although it's a bit like learning how to count in the same lesson as you're being taught advanced mathematics. Still, if you're happy with the devil and the deep blue sea. We'll vote on it.'

In the end spelling was outvoted on the basis that it was an aboriginal subject, and a compromise was made on a grammar component. Mr Harrison crumpled in tears that he could just hold back in a scowl. He would be stuck loading trucks for the rest of his life because the stupid bitch up front would not teach him how to spell, how to fill out a requisition form. These other people had come along with nothing at stake. Mrs White, it was obvious, had come for an interest. They had no shame, none of them, to cut him out and destroy his life to suit themselves. He wanted to hit somebody, to punch that woman until she looked like a casserole. Coon classes. He wasn't a coon. How dare she imply there was black blood in him, that he should go to coon classes and learn how to spell. Tomorrow they would be loading two dogs, and the cops would be stalking round for their money, and he would have to drive a load that would peel him like a banana if he stopped short down a hill. And there was that Jones bastard that checked off the times, and filled out the forms, and never so much as caught a crab off a gearstick with his automatic Holden and his easy overtime. If only he had the words and the ways that pleased a boss. But a pencil wouldn't sit behind his cauliflower ear, and this bitch was here to tell him. She couldn't be more than twenty.

'I've brought in a Ray Bradbury short story, "The Scythe". I thought we could discuss it, as an introduction to literature.'

'Scythe?' asked somebody. 'Isn't that a kind of a lathe?'

Lucy drew a picture of the instrument on the blackboard.

'It's a new moon,' one of the women interrupted.

'No,' said Lucy, 'it's death. Has it got a sharp or blunt edge?'

'You mean dying slowly or painfully,' said Mrs White. 'But it's got a handle. I don't see why the moon's got a handle.'

'It's a sword, isn't it?'

'Yes,' answered Lucy.

'Like the sword Arabs use to cut off testicles,' said one of the men who had voted for spelling.

'You mean,' said Lucy, 'that death is the infidel.'

'No,' said the man, blushing. 'My wife's an infidel. I'm getting a divorce so she can marry him, all she likes.'

'Let's read the story then,' said Lucy, wishing she could be left alone to the insects. It would be easier teaching a mosquito not to suck blood than to cosset humans into learning.

'Man arrives at deserted farmhouse,' she said, summarising, simplifying with the heaving efforts of a weightlifter, 'finds a house in good order, and a glistening knife for harvesting wheat. Every time he cuts the wheat to a stubble, more comes up, until he realises that this is not good fortune, that he is killing people. He can hear their voices.'

'He must be mad,' said a young woman, 'hearing voices.'

'No,' said Lucy, 'he realises that he has unwittingly become death, has been seduced into the most terrible kind of immortality. One day he must hear the voices of his wife and the children he loves, and he must kill them. He must kill them because he is death.'

'I think it's a disgusting story,' said Mrs White. 'There's too much violence altogether in the world today. Last week, at the open-air cinema, I saw a film about a man who murders his wife and children just because they wanted him to get a promotion. First he gets his wife and singes the hair on her arms, and he makes the children watch, and they seem to be enjoying it, and then he takes off her eyebrows. I think he was using a soldering torch. After that he cuts off her hair and burns it in a cornflakes bowl on the table and . . .'

Lucy laughed. 'Which is funnier, do you think, slapstick violence or slapstick humour? Or are they the same?'

'I saw the film,' said one of the other women. 'I thought she got what was coming to her.'

Lucy groaned faintly. Perhaps she was getting what she deserved, coming to a small town and expecting people to understand her. It was only in big cities that people favoured the newcomer, fleeced her of her ideas and then sent her scudding home with a yawn.

She began to discuss symbolism, a central symbol, like a scythe cutting itself through the story valiantly, swimming through the novel like a fish, until it is finally caught. A fish out of water, suffocating in the air that is realism. Nobody understood, and she didn't either, not when faced with their begrudging silence, the chalk bone powder that clung like a shroud around her fingers.

'Excuse me.' Titus had given her no idea that he intended coming to class. 'I'm sorry I'm late. I hope I haven't missed too much.'

'It's a Tuesday, mate,' said Mr Harrison, as if the ghost of his own failure had come to claim his soul. 'You'll be wanting the literacy classes. There'll be no writing or spelling, mate. We've voted on it, savvy, voted. Ask the caretaker, he'll tell you where to be going.'

'I'm sorry,' said Titus, 'I don't understand what you're saying. I've enrolled in an English literature course, haven't I?'

'Yes,' smiled Lucy gratefully, 'as Mr Harrison has just said, we voted on it.'

To have the hostility directed away from herself would make it easier to teach. She had never been as pleased to see anybody in her whole life. He could be as unfriendly as he liked after this.

'We were discussing symbolism,' said Lucy, 'in a short story. I was hoping to get the students to write a story, a page or so, using a central symbol. A butterfly to represent freedom, a candle, life, a white flower, innocence, a beer can, impotence. Anything, can't you see, anything can equal anything.'

In the case of certain students, anything was equal to nothing. But two people wrote furiously, laughing louder, as it were, because they couldn't understand the joke. Lucy smiled to herself and remembered times at school when Suzie and Mavis had told her a dirty joke and she'd laughed her head off, only to find out that the punch line had been false.

She felt sorry she had disappointed them. They had come to class expecting so much. They had placed their money on the direction the ant would travel. What could she do but throw up ideas, build their egos a little?

'I'd like you to read what you've written, Mrs White.'

Mrs White had been writing furiously, one plain, one

purl, with admirable concentration.

'I chose the candle as my symbol,' she said, quickly turning to face the class, small-boned and eager as a rat expecting a fight. 'It isn't cruel because the candle cries tears of wax until the person's life is over.'

'The candle is death?' asked Lucy.

'Of course,' said Mrs White.

'And Mr Harrison.'

'I've only written a few lines,' he said, 'but I see death as a truck. When you carry a heavy load you speed it down a hill, but slow it on its way up.'

'That's very good,' said Lucy. 'I'm pleased you have both got the idea.'

'If that's all a symbol's about, then I'm laughing,' said Mr Harrison. 'I wish I could put them on requisition forms.'

'I've used a stone,' said Titus, 'like the others for a symbol of death. It is a tool, and it can be sharpened. It can live under water or in the air. People kick stones, yet have an urge to follow their path. They can be weapons, decorations for the grave, magic turingas for healing. We are a "stone age" people because our ancestors have turned to stone. We can't chisel out a shape we have guessed for them and call it Art.'

'That's a strange thing for an artist to say,' said Lucy.

'I record rather than change. To be an artist is a half-caste's punishment. If I'd been truly of my tribe they would have made me into a sorcerer, with the power of life and death. But how can I be trusted, except as a scribe, a spear decorator, the purveyor of accepted secrets with the taint of what is really secret. I'm like a blackmailer who has to provide only the whiff of a suggestion to get payment, the attention of my people who are afraid for what I will betray to the whites.'

'I think you are being too hard on yourself,' said Lucy, forgetting about the others, swotting insects and rustling paper as if it were new currency in their hands.

'I'm harder on others,' he said calmly.

'Then that's the limit. We're all becoming so bloody choosy, no one's ready to do the work,' said Mr Harrison. 'Although some people have never worked.'

Titus lowered his head. He seemed to be inviting their abuse, not from a desire for self-destruction, but rather, and she couldn't quite believe it, from an acceptance of the class, her family of intolerable relatives who had imposed themselves on him for the occasion. She felt grateful, elated. He could put up with what she could not.

'It's very interesting, our discussion,' said one of the quieter women. 'But I was wondering why writers need symbols. I mean death is death and a candle is a candle.'

'It's as simple as one and one making two,' said Lucy. 'But a symbol can make you take on another life. It's like playing at dressing up, when you attempt to deceive yourself, not others. It's not a disguise you see.'

'When I was down in Adelaide,' said Mr Harrison, 'I laid into some of those men who dress up in women's clothing. We were in this bar, and somebody had to tell us what they were. So we followed them and ripped off their sheilas' clothing, and I took one of their wigs home for me missus. She was real pleased.'

'I didn't mean anything like that,' said Lucy, looking upwards to the fan, hoping its slow jerking movements would crank up her enthusiasm for her class. 'Have you ever wanted to be something, someone else? More importantly, have you ever not wanted to be someone?'

'I'm glad I'm not a coon,' said Mr Harrison. 'No offence to anyone present. I've never wanted to be a coon. Funny thing that is, I've never thought about being a coon until now. You'd think I might have had a nightmare once in my life, but I've never given them much thought. I didn't think I'd come to class to learn about being a coon. I didn't think literature would be depressing, but that's life, isn't it? Depressing. If I'd wanted a good time I could have gone to the Memorial Club.'

There was something soothing about Mr Harrison's frankness, thought Lucy, like the rough openness of the sea, unpalatable, unpredictable, unlikeable. But other members of the class, the small craft, were sailing the surface of his prejudice, pirates hoping to profit from their risk. Their eyes showed an investment of sparkle, of interest as he spoke his thoughts wildly.

'I didn't mean to make my story depressing,' said Mrs White, hoping to gain his acceptance in spite of earlier disagreement. She had decided that Mr Harrison would not be outvoted on further issues. 'I suppose that literature has its darker side, like anything else.'

'Yes,' said Lucy, 'perhaps that's something we could discuss next Thursday, the darker side of literature.'

She desperately wanted to laugh, to write a letter to Adelaide to clarify her emotions. It would be a nice, safe kind of letter, secured by her growing regard for Titus.

The caretaker was outside the classroom, waiting for his key. He had taken one look at Lucy and realised that she could never be trusted to return it. Younger every year, he thought, they migrated from the south with their ideas, but all they ever ended up doing was mating. And that was natural. He would have been in there too like a shot with this new one, if he had his teeth and a good back.

Alice Springs

Dear Adelaide,

Farewell to Old Sydney forever. I write to you, friend, in the hope of a new life, that you find within yourself the grace to overlook my misfortune, that society will one day curtail its wrath.

I have been transported to this new world where there are no seasons as we were used. Where a number of miserable market gardens constitute the town agriculture. It is a dangerous place, full of thieves and pickpockets who own large and ill-defined tracts of land wherein they graze cattle and all manner of poachables. My head is spinning.

I have made myself a widow's cap to gain respectability, and carry with me a pistol as was my manner when you knew me. I think of you often my dearest friend. Do not attempt a visit before winter. The devil himself leaves for cooler climes at this time.

I remain your aff. etc. servant etc., Lucy.

Dear Adelaide,

Let me begin over again. I want you to understand, if you can, how different it is here. The country is rich, like a bright stage set, full of trapdoors for the unwary. The sun creates the unnatural heat of footlights. I feel that I am constantly being watched, that I'm about to make a great error and that the audience will stampede me in order to get back their money. For one thing, my first class was a disaster. I mean we had no basis on which to communicate. Matthew's brother is in the class, and if it weren't for him, but that's another matter.

I haven't seen a fence since I got up here, except in the town. But there are several boundaries set out in trespass notices published weekly in the paper. One can imagine an innocent party having a picnic on those stations, miscalculating a boundary on their topographical maps and being shot.

Violence here is as thick as the dust. People are puffed out with it, blown about no matter how much their hush puppies attempt to anchor them. They wear their long socks like poultices, in anticipation of injury. You will see them in their tropical bermudas when you come to visit.

By the time you arrive, the trees will be all cut down. It is like the Passover, only the trees marked with the red crosses will not be spared. All this is very appropriate, as it is hell, here, in the heat. All things Christian are inverted, like they are in a black mass (or a white mass, as it would be here).

Titus has a friend who's a priest. I met him yesterday. I didn't shudder or make mental confessions to myself, or count the countless Sundays I've abstained from communion. I looked him straight in the eye, pagan and brazen, and felt from that instant he was human, that his doubts had to be greater than mine because he needed a church to shore them up. He seemed like a body buried alive between church walls. A dissenter made great because he was fighting, fighting doubts with all his might, struggling for his last breath in that cavity between walls.

Before Matthew goes out to Papunya for his operations, he's going to take me and Esther (his mother) to Glen Helen. Esther is an exceptional person. Very strong and independent, with lots of ideas. In many ways she is the antithesis of Mum. I wonder what they'd think of one another if they met. I don't think Mum would like her fighting, but I think you'd like her, I think you two might get along. Anyway I'll send you some photos so you'll have some idea of the place. It's quite strange living in a small town. Already some of the town faces have begun to repeat themselves. I think of Mussolini slyly marching the same troops around the block and back again into the parade to impress Hitler. I'm not impressed by these recycled phantoms with their trumped-up whiteness.

This is, so far, what I have to say. I will write soon.
Lucy

She lay back, thankfully, onto a cool bed. Her first class was over, she had re-established contact with Adelaide, and she had time now to think. She no longer felt confused. The past seemed to be loosening its grip, as if she had found a new protector.

Titus had chosen to come to class. What a strange name it was – Titus. Chosen by his father? She conjured the image of a white witchety-grub male digging itself into the black earth to be disgorged in a new generation. The new, diluted generation. It was there for the world to contemplate.

Diluted food could at least be enjoyed by children, by a delicate palate. Children preferred watered milk, or watered tea. As people got older they drank their tea stronger, but it could never taste as good as it did when they were small and held the first pale cup to their mouths. Hard black absolutes came with age, nuns, death. Now she wanted to forget them. Black and white were relevant when they crossed over, like chromosomes. People with pedigrees, she imagined, were little use to anyone. They had to look for things to be brave about, like small poodles sniffing out adventure in parks, or tired old ladies with secret letters.

She admired Titus. Perhaps he had only come to class because he felt sorry for her, or for Matthew's sake. They were a close family, but she hoped his motivation was different.

Drowsiness, the south-west slopes. Dams brown thirst quenching, sheep white absorbent standing in the shade of trees. She had taken so much for granted then, as now sleep was taking her for granted in its obstinate way.

8

'This is Namatjira country,' said Matthew, taking the four-wheel drive off the main road in the direction of Mount Sonder. 'Can you see the outline of the sleeping woman?

'She's always painted with ghost gums in the foreground,' said Titus to Lucy. 'Protected by phantoms. You've seen those Rex Battarbee colours, lurid and watery.'

'Namatjira was a full blood of the Aranda tribe,' said Esther. 'I knew him. I knew him well when I used to camp at Hermannsburg Mission.'

Esther, Titus and Lucy bounced from spring to spring inside the vehicle, their heads hitting the roof of the cabin.

'Albert was a full blood who painted like a half-caste,' said Titus. 'I'm a half-caste trying to paint like a full blood, with ochre, string, blood, hair. Ironically, it's the half-caste painting which is more highly regarded.'

'We had a good time when Albert made that money,' said Esther. 'He shared it round. Most of it went on drink. I told him to use it sensibly, so there'd be alcohol for longer, but it was drunk so bloody quickly it did him in. It might do Keith in if he's not careful, living in his brother's shadow.' Esther took in a deep breath. 'What my people have got to learn is how to do themselves in more slowly, not go too wildly under, like dogs on a public roadway.'

'Very true,' said Titus, who'd resolved never to drink. 'A lot of responsibility rested on Albert.'

'He never gave his wives enough credit,' said Esther. 'He was a good man, so they didn't ask for it. You know, Lucy, it was the women who did his drawings. He later painted them up with white man's colours. I think he did try to tell the experts from the south that his wives had helped, but they got angry and didn't want to know about it. After that he used to say to us it was taboo for white women to paint. So we all had to keep quiet. Poor old Albert, he didn't have one of those good brains. We liked him though.'

'Didn't they put him into prison for alcohol?' asked Lucy.

'His sentence got commuted,' said Titus. 'I remember when I was little, he showed me a photograph of his mother. She was in harness, pulling some cattle feed into a station. If only he could have painted her, rather than this docile brumby of a Mount Sonder on her back.'

'Why didn't he?' asked Lucy, fascinated by Titus, his mixture of intelligence and passion which seemed to tame the landscape.

'He couldn't,' replied Titus, 'because his mother wasn't dead long enough. Until an ancestor is well and truly dead, mythical if you like, she can't be painted. It would have been extremely shameful for Albert to bring his mother's image back to life in harness.'

'Yes,' affirmed Esther. 'But it would never have occurred to him to do it.'

'Now a respectable time has passed,' said Titus, 'I've done a painting of her. It's called "The Artist's Mother Finds An Occupation".'

'Can I see it?' asked Lucy eagerly.

'Someone in Adelaide bought it,' said Matthew. 'That's why Titus could afford his car.'

'But wouldn't Namatjira have destroyed the photograph once his mother died?' asked Lucy.

'He was drinking too much,' said Esther, 'and he

wanted to punish himself. There are many reasons why people don't behave according to custom.'

'Will you destroy the picture of father,' said Matthew, 'when he dies?'

'No,' laughed Esther. 'He's a white man. A ghost that'd forgotten almost everything when I met him. He'll give me no trouble when he goes. There'll be no rough transitions.'

Lucy felt the importance of Esther's words. Rough transitions. It was the fulcrum which was the least jarring. The point of balance in a see-saw, the meeting of cultures, love midway between extremities. Desire held at the body's gravitational centre, not trusted to the toes. As a child she'd prayed to be taken out of life smoothly. She had placed no trust in gentle transitions when too much of the world had seemed harsh, striated, like bird sound, with each season clamouring to be the next. Now perhaps she would come to understand the country, its gentleness. Titus would give it depth and perspective.

'Some people give mobs of trouble after they die,' continued Esther. 'Usually the ones who are difficult while they live. They get jealous, revengeful, even if they get the right burial, and everyone puts in a lot of time on the ceremony, and you wear their bones until you hear them rattling in your sleep. There was one man, for example, out at Yuendumu, who killed two people for eating his favourite plant, even though at the time he was in the land of the dead. He got jealous of them having something he couldn't enjoy eating for himself anymore. But after a while they forget. They all forget, which is only natural, isn't it?'

'Yes,' agreed Lucy, looking at the steep sides of Glen Helen Gorge. 'Is this water hole permanent?'

'As permanent as Sydney Harbour,' smiled Matthew.

Esther, who couldn't swim, went in knee deep.

'It seems a shame to swim in good drinking water,' she

shouted, turning her back to them and standing as still as the cliffs.

The others followed. The water was new melted ice, making the blue of the sky jump into their veins. Lucy had never felt such a contrast before, when only a moment ago she'd felt weak and sick from the heat. Dangerously alive, she feared her body would start to twitch uncontrollably.

'This is beautiful,' she said to Matthew, 'but I think the water's already giving me a cramp. My foot's starting to hurt.'

'Get out,' said Matthew. 'If it's too cold, get out.'

'It's so painful,' cried Lucy, attempting to untangle her frozen muscles and tendons, allowing Matthew to rub the instep of her foot. 'That's helping,' she said.

'You should eat more salt,' said Matthew. 'The heat can take it out of your body, especially here, and give you cramps.'

Titus came out of the water. He seemed put out that Matthew's treatment was working. He watched them with embarrassing concentration, surprised that he hadn't been consulted.

'She must drink the water,' he said. 'There's enough salt in it. Stretch her foot as far as it'll go.'

He took her foot from Matthew and began to straighten it with the palms of his hands. It was a reassuring action. The warmth from his hands brought relief and pleasure as he found the gaps between her toes.

She began to warm in the sun, her foot almost better. Titus was allowing rather polite spaces of time between the pressure of his hands. He seemed afraid to look at her. Lucy, feeling desire too strongly to remain calm, went back into the water to join Esther.

'My husband,' said Mrs Hayes, who had remained in the same position, facing away from them, 'spent time up north. He had a woman there.' She looked up to the top of the break in the folds of delicate sandstone. It was a dramatic cut, rising red and arrogant out of the level ranges. 'She taught him one of her tribe's songs. It's the one I like best, and I think Titus likes it too.' She looked meaningfully at Lucy, and like a pelican, leg stalks half in water, she began to sing, moving rhythmically, without seeming to disturb the water.

> Stars are close-feathered
> balls on a string
> Rising, feathers of light they fling
> on water
> cross water
> on seagulls' wings.
>
> Seagull, spoonbill, feathers for a star
> made by a maker Maingalma
> whose ghost hands clap like sticks
> as he makes,
> whose ghost friends lift their arms
> as they dance
> fingernails hooked into darkness
> as they dance
> Dance their wild dance on Caledon Bay.
>
> Maingalma puts short string to feather
> strings to mainlength lightly,
> those which will flower nightly.
> His pack-feather will flower nightly
> in Baleibalei.
>
> The spoonbill stars follow the water
> made by a maker Maingalma.
> His ghost hands clap to the
> dance he is making,
> His ghost friends lift their arms
> as they dance
> clap to the song of daylight breaking.

> Morning star,
> hangs from a tree
> a star on a string
> at Baleibalei.

She'd recited the northern poem to Lucy to prove her tolerance of different tribes, cultures. But Lucy was left unsure. Every object had competing connotations. Feathers were clouds, feathered string could be a love token or a funeral decoration. And there was the magic spider string that a sorceror used to pull himself up into the sky to deal with spirits. So she decided to take the most favourable interpretation, imagining the star as a love token, scattering feathers of light and hope through the world.

Esther showed no surprise at the period of silence which had passed between them. It was not insulting to have a companion who wanted to think.

'I'm going to light a fire,' she said. 'By the time it gets going the sun will be cooler.'

Esther went off to gather wood beyond the rich afternoon redness of the cliffs, beyond the feathery shadows of trees. There was plenty of wood to choose from, in shapes that had been burnt and reburnished over time. A banquet of history. Fireside gossip locked into wood, released again as ash, part of a face in mourning, a rubbing to stop an initiation scar from healing over.

She lay a pile of wood on the sand, selected for shape, burning properties. The shape was important. If she selected a piece like the face of a dog, it might remind certain spirits she knew of the time they were alive and their pet dog was eaten. It would also be unwise to burn the snake. It was a sacred totem. Unfortunately, Esther laughed to herself, so many pieces of wood were shaped that way, it appeared to be a show of strength on the part of the rainbow serpent, a curse on fire-builders like herself.

'And tell me, Lucy, about your country,' said Esther, with the security of a wood gatherer who had a large pile of wood beside her. 'I never got to visit Matthew when he was down in your country.'

'It's not really mine,' smiled Lucy. 'Once my country was Ireland. But everyone in a city has a different country.'

'It sounds like a settlement,' said Esther. 'Maybe Papunya, or Utopia, or Warrabri, where people have been brought together from different tribes. Is there much petrol sniffing that goes on in Sydney?'

'Not much voluntary petrol sniffing,' laughed Lucy. 'But perhaps it's not very different from a reservation.'

'There's a lot of fighting that goes on in settlements,' said Esther. 'Maybe Matthew won't be able to operate on the blind men. He'll be too busy looking after the others.'

'I don't think they spend all their time fighting,' said Matthew impatiently, ashamed of his mother. She was always talking on that subject. 'Although I don't want Lucy to think that settlements are good places. They aren't.'

'You should see the women out there,' said Mrs Hayes. 'You can't stop them. They'll pick up a nulla nulla and crack it over the skull of the first man that comes along.'

'Don't exaggerate,' said Matthew, uneasily. 'You'll mislead Lucy. We're speaking of inter-tribal problems.'

'Women have a right to use their nulla nullas,' laughed Titus. 'According to the law it was they who created the world, gave birth to men, and administered the law until men stole it from them during the dreamtime.'

'You're right,' said Esther sadly, regretting her son had not become a sorcerer. He went for the truth on such a clean track. 'We had all the power once.'

'If men don't keep their secrets from women,' said Titus, 'the women will regain their power. A corroboree, you know, reinstates a man. It acts out the birth process while telling stories of female power and the way the secrets of that power were captured from them. Sometimes before the beginning of the dance, a man has to steal something from a woman, something only a woman is allowed to make. In Arnhem Land they steal string.'

'So I give Henry a hiding when I feel like it,' said Esther with satisfaction.

'Your sex is in exile,' smiled Titus, 'like I was when I was down in Adelaide looking for work.'

'We have our own corroborees,' said Esther. 'The fact that the men are thieves gives us privileges, pride.'

'Do you ever want to get your old power back?' asked Lucy.

'No,' said Esther. 'Men got the better of us in the dreamtime when the laws were made. But they have to live with their shame.'

'You don't feel inferior?' said Lucy.

'Inferior,' laughed Esther. 'The person who's inferior is the one who breaks the law.'

'But if you had to choose between being a man and a woman,' asked Lucy, 'which would you choose?'

'I'd choose to be a woman,' she said, taking on the warmth of the fire. 'A woman's stronger. She does the hand-to-hand combat. You get more strength from fighting that way than from using spears. Also a woman can eat every day; a man has to wait to gorge himself after the hunt.'

'I suppose it's the difference between a permanent and casual job,' said Matthew. 'But hunting would be less boring, wouldn't it?'

'I don't know,' said Esther. 'I catch snakes. They're more dangerous than kangaroos. If you want excitement you can go looking for it. But I don't enjoy men's hunting. I've done it once or twice. You have to depend on others. Besides, there aren't many good hunters left.'

'But there are some,' said Titus, searching the cliffs for

the faces of famous ancestors. 'Old Jabadi, for example, he can make himself look and sound just like an animal. He can become so like one of them that he will decide not to kill. He's a brilliant tracker, will follow tracks for days, predicting where the animal will go by looking at its excrement, then telling by that how fast or slow it's been travelling, and whether or not he has a chance of catching up.'

'He is someone special,' said Esther. 'I knew him when he was a little feller. But I was never one of those who went after the big hunters. Preened up like sportsmen, they could do their killing in half the time if they didn't have to think about their reputations.'

Lucy laughed loudly. Esther looked confused by this. Eucalyptus leaves crackled in the fire, blessing with their sweet incense the profanity of someone caught between two cultures, two walls.

Titus looked intensely at Lucy. He was worried by her laughter. It seemed to him rather abstract and cruel. Or perhaps, which was more insulting, she was laughing at Esther. His uncertainty showed by the way he stoked the fire, exposing the wood slowly and despondently, then allowing it to drop back suddenly and splinter into flames.

When Lucy realised that she'd offended him she became afraid. Her expression grew serious.

'I'm sorry,' she said. 'I'm not laughing at you. But at everything. Today it's been like someone speaking my own language with a different accent. It's likeable, funny. You have a different accent. The Australian accent. I feel out of place, not inferior. Do you understand?'

'Don't feel out of place,' said Titus, looking intensely at her. 'Amongst the Aranda you are either totally accepted or not. And only a certain number of allowances will be made either way.'

'Accepted totally?' repeated Lucy with the hesitation of someone who had never felt wanted, with the strong desire of it.

'Yes,' said Titus, turning over the coals. 'Totally.'

This private conversation angered Matthew. He hadn't expected disloyalty from his brother. There was a physical closeness between Titus and Lucy. They had no right to it.

'I think we should be going home soon,' he said angrily. 'Lucy looks sunburnt. The sun can't be agreeing with her.'

'It's agreeing with me,' said Lucy happily. 'It really is.'

'Tell the truth,' said Matthew.

'I'm trying to,' said Lucy.

'Anyway I've got to get back,' he said abruptly. 'I've got things to organise.'

'Yes,' said Titus, looking apologetically at Matthew. 'It would be an idea to get back.'

'That's if Lucy doesn't mind,' said Matthew, trying to hide the hostility in his voice. 'Perhaps you two can come here again while I'm in Papunya.'

Esther looked away. There were times when she regretted Matthew taking up the scholarship. It had made him jealous of white approval. Of course it was all right to look for their acceptance. Hadn't she done exactly that? But to be disappointed when acceptance went to another member of the family, that was dangerous. He should know what happens to tribes that start to break up. Spirits could come to widen the cracks until they were canyons wide enough to fall between. Glen Helen Gorge had been split a long time ago. But it was a warning now to her sons not to be separated, not to make a distance between themselves that others could drink from. She did not believe that Lucy was deliberately attempting to divide them. But she had that thirst, the thirst of someone white who is first in the desert; the desperation which watches a deep pool of water dry up in a day, leaving its hollow of clay disfigured for accepting in the first place the gift of rain.

There were no real gifts in the desert, merely those necessities which pleased and those which displeased. Even a permanent water hole could dry up. She had nothing against Lucy. She liked her. But the poor girl would be in for some surprises. Matthew should have helped her understand, not think of love. As for Titus, he was being even more reckless than his brother. She could see how deeply he cared for Lucy.

Luckily, Matthew had obligations in Papunya. For once she was grateful to that place, its inhuman desolation, the young boys with petrol pumps half up their noses. He needed time alone with his people. Time to put whites into perspective. Titus was already too much in love to be helped. She packed slowly. If it came to a fight she'd have to call in some of her relatives. If it came to a fight all would be lost.

On the way home, in the thickness of animal life brought by twilight, Esther's thoughts groped for space. Matthew didn't care enough for anyone. He was refined, cautious. Like all precious objects, he would not allow himself to be misused. He wanted to be respected by whites as was his due. He had the cool, tempered expectancy of a nobleman.

Titus was different. He had strong feelings, was ready to be humiliated for what he believed in. He was too close to the Aranda, to the old order. When she considered things more closely, she could place a certain amount of hope in Lucy, that she would put him more in touch with the new order. It was not necessarily wrong to trust a white. Her husband had behaved himself well, respected her ways. Change could happen when there was respect on both sides, when it was not obligatory. Obligatory change rarely lasted longer than it took the obligation to be understood.

Titus had never been close to anyone but herself. People were afraid of him. They said there was too much secrecy, stored like eggs under his skin, ready to hatch with the first good season. Many feared his unused power. Feared the artist that dealt in secrets, holding the truth over his people as a punishment.

Birds and insects had begun to follow the currents of air around their vehicle.

'I'll drive carefully,' said Matthew uneasily as two slow-feathered owls hit the windscreen, one soon after the other.

'Be careful,' said Lucy, hesitantly. 'We're all vulnerable at dusk when it's time to feed.'

The bush seemed to be coming in closer, surrounding their thoughts. It was like an animal listening to itself eat, and it had a rather self-conscious urgency about it, a knowledge of the night.

'I shouldn't be desperate,' thought Lucy, listening to each twig snap in the darkness. 'In the morning it'll all look the same, in spite of the foraging. There is room for everyone, for Titus and me to enjoy ourselves unnoticed.'

She concentrated on the way his shoulders remained straight as he sat forward; straight, square, with an occasional nervous movement to acknowledge her watching. There was little doubt in her mind now she would have to let him know her feelings, how she needed his regard to disprove her past: to absolve the mother who let people use affections like a pack of cards, for Reg the joker banished from the pack, and for poor, crepuscular de Bosco, God's debt collector. It was almost dark now. The bush was quiet, a well-fed animal preening itself under the cold fire of stars.

9

Matthew had been away three weeks in Papunya and some of the remote surrounding districts. It had been a quiet time for Lucy, her impressions in the February heat soaring upwards and away in the manner of balloons she had not had time to paint a face on. The air-conditioner was broken down, and Titus's friend, Father Vivian Scarf, in the thudding abstraction of temperatures in the forties, was intent upon conversation.

'When I saw you last time,' he said, 'I didn't tell you about the new church. I've been promised fifty per cent.'

'Are you pleased?' asked Lucy, looking into his tabby-green eyes, avoiding the electrocuted streaks in his thin red beard.

'Not really,' he said. 'It means I'm going to be incredibly busy making up the difference. "Thou shalt be busy, yet thou shalt not covet thy neighbour's business."'

'Then you've come to the wrong house,' laughed Lucy. 'Here we're as idle as Carmelites.'

'That's exactly what I need,' he said with relief. 'Exactly.'

'It's a shame,' said Lucy, 'you can't marry Christ like a nun can. Then you'd be able to lead the life of a bored and idle Five Dock housewife.'

'What are you talking about?' he laughed. He'd become informal with Titus's friend. They'd had good talks together.

'I went to school in Five Dock,' she said. 'The nuns used to say they were married to Christ. Marriage was the only respectable state for women then. So they were God's housewives, keeping up appearances, reading the Mills and Boon romances of the lives of the saints, forgetting the hard village lives they'd left in Ireland.'

The priest looked at her sharply. 'You can offer idleness to God,' he said. 'Unemployment, idleness, whatever. To do nothing in someone's presence is a greater compliment than being busy and preoccupied.'

'Provided it's not a coin tied to a string,' said Lucy. 'Here is the contribution that is really meant for my pocket.'

'Perhaps human beings should be measured by the length of string they choose,' said Father Scarf. 'We attach strings to everything, especially the bargains we make with God.'

He stood up nervously as if to leave. Then sat down again. The young girl interested him.

'I gave a sermon last week,' he said, smiling. 'But you haven't come yet, have you? On self-interest. I used the rich man and Lazarus. I said the rich man today would have thrown Lazarus some scraps of food, not out of the goodness of his heart but out of the strictness of his diet.'

'Does that constitute progress?' laughed Lucy.

'I think we can speak of material progress,' he said, 'even in matters of selfishness.'

'So the Church like a true multinational is diversifying out of the spiritual world.'

'If you want to speak in those terms,' he said, 'the Church has always been juggling the material and the spiritual.'

'Just as you need to talk to a lapsed Catholic like me,' she interrupted, 'to bolster your belief.'

'Perhaps you're right,' he laughed. 'There's nothing like a heretic to kindle religious fire.'

'I don't see myself as a disbeliever,' she said. 'In that sense I suppose I'm a true heretic.'

'Worth burning,' he said. 'The desert doesn't reward defiance.'

'Nor did the nuns,' she laughed.

'It's more dangerous here than you think,' he said. 'You're a white woman living in this house.'

'I know it's dangerous,' said Lucy. 'But the heat keeps me punch drunk, feeling happy and invulnerable. Intellectually I know there are enemies about.'

'There are,' he said with conviction.

'What can I do?' she asked.

'Run away,' he replied. 'Go with Titus. Leave the hate and don't look back.'

'Like Mrs Lot,' smiled Lucy.

'Exactly,' he said. 'I know the mentality of this town. It's the town which feeds me.' He made jerking movements hand to beard, like a dog with fleas. 'It feeds me in the same way as it supports its community organisations. I am Lions, Rotary, Apex all put together. And then it passes round the plate, so the businessmen can watch one another for the size of the contributions they make. Mine host I am to their money. Rosy cheeked I wait at the cash register. Hospitable too, because I have eaten early. I fold napkins under their chins and they become gods inside. They sing and praise my management, the way I have handled the Mass. Until some uninvited black comes drunk and unsteady to the table. Or a woman wears a short skirt. And the men would rather she be unleavened under their weight than pretend she needs soul yeast.'

Lucy felt his passion. She could understand why Titus liked him. 'The man with the bushfire beard' as he called him. Burnt out it was like a stretch of scrub in bits of black and tobacco-brown. He was, in his way, the sign that things could get no worse, a sign more potent than a rainbow.

'And you know about the trees,' he said irrelevantly.

'It's such a terrible shame. I love those cedars. Three weeks ago I read them the psalm about the cedars of Lebanon, hoping they would take the hint. But the crosses appeared not long after.

'They're going to replace them with root-bound eucalypts in concrete tubs. The more concrete the better; the more sub-contracting of cheap labour the more the council pays the full price to somebody's cousin.'

'In a small town corruption bubbles to the surface, bubbles and blisters,' said Lucy, looking hopefully towards the air-conditioner. 'But perhaps there'll be a cooling-down time one day.'

'It'll never be cool enough,' said the priest. 'There are a number of people in town who have come specifically to cool off. Some of the police have criminal records. The wealthiest man here is wanted by the New York Mafia. They have all come to cool down, to escape into petty crime. Ironically it's the next-door neighbours, the respectable itinerants from cities who, in the difficulty of the weather, murder each other.'

'And there is the tribal violence as well,' said Lucy. 'Why are you building another church? To keep the two societies separate?'

'The aborigines should have their own place to worship,' said the priest, 'where they can take Holy Communion according to their consciences. It's a transient society here. Black and white nomads trying not to cross paths, dreaming tracks if you like. Public servants on transfer, Pitjinjarra men tolerated on Aranda territory, Walbiris come to visit. It is a series of easements and concessions that form a loose woven bag. The black race is used to this pattern. The white isn't.

'Would you like a beer?' asked the priest. 'Titus keeps it in the fridge for visitors.' His awkward shark's mouth played with the authority of an invitation. 'Sometimes I need a drink, so I can forget that my parishioners are getting drunk.' He went to the kitchen. 'Why did you come here?' he asked, looking into the refrigerator.

They were interrupted when Titus walked into the room with a shoebox under his arm.

'Locusts?' asked Lucy, excitedly. She ran over to the box with its ragged sky holes. 'Can I have a look?'

'It's a lizard,' he said. 'It's a kind that doesn't taste any good.'

He took off the lid of the shoebox to reveal a little dragon in its corner, with an armour of thorn and slow stupid eyes.

'Are those spikes poisonous?' she asked. 'Will it jump out at me?'

'Moloch horridus,' said the priest in Latin voice.

'No,' smiled Titus at Lucy. 'The spikes aren't even sharp.'

'A Moloch horridus won't hurt you,' agreed the priest.

'Hold out your hand,' said Titus. He placed the delicate piece of medievalism on her hand, stroking it gently.

'Can you feel anything happening?' asked the priest. 'Some animals have spurs that secrete moisture.'

'No,' said Lucy. 'It feels ticklish and light, like a feather. It's just like a feather.'

'A feather?' asked Titus, wondering if Lucy understood the significance of what she was saying, feeling a burst of optimism.

'Yes,' she said, 'that's it exactly. He's a beautiful creature.'

'I had a pet locust,' said the priest. 'I made a leash for it out of cotton.'

'I knew someone who used to pull their wings off before racing them,' said Lucy, watching Titus stroking the underbelly of the reptilian battering ram. 'I remember he gave me one once. There was still a little bit left. One torn wing, ragged and veined on either side in perfect co-ordination.'

'The locust was the playground sub-species,' the priest explained. 'The problem was it did nothing when it was caught, spun no silk, ate no sugar, stung no sting.'

'This one doesn't do much either,' said Titus, 'except camouflage.'

'What's that lump on its back?' asked Lucy, wanting to be alone with Titus.

'Food, ' he said. 'It's also a decoy. When a predator comes towards it, it attacks what is really just a lump on top of its body. His real head's tucked safely underneath.'

'That's very two-faced of him,' laughed the priest.

'He's able to stay still most of the time,' said Titus, 'for camouflage. He can soak up water through his legs, and drink it when it's near to his mouth.'

'I wonder,' said Lucy, 'if this little dinosaur in days gone by shrank from standing too long in lakes. I can see it stranded pre-Pleistocene, waiting patiently for the water to travel that immense distance up to its mouth.'

'What a wonderful image,' said the priest. 'He's difficult to see on this speckledy carpet,' said Lucy. 'I wonder if he would roll into a ball if I stroked him the right way.'

'He's the lizard that eats five thousand ants at one meal,' said the priest. 'But he has weak jaws. It's difficult to imagine, isn't it?'

'Do your jaws get weak from Sunday sermons?' smiled Titus, wondering if the man would take the hint, and leave.

The expression on Vivian Scarf's face changed. He had a changeable face, which in between alarming moments could appear serene and immobile. Perhaps, thought Titus, it had something to do with the sudden doubts which beset him like flash floods, reducing him to temporary disarray and confusion. But these, in spite of the devastation they caused, seemed essential to his internal balance.

'I'd rather be a lizard than a priest,' the priest said bitterly. Titus's remark had set him thinking. 'I wouldn't have to go to the local businessmen to get my ants.'

'The idea is to pray for the salvation of their souls,' said Lucy. 'That is the best way to resolve your contempt. Take their money, wish them better. Take it. Turn it into bricks and altars and white linen cloth.'

'You're right,' said Vivian, turning rapidly to leave.

Lucy looked sympathetically at the priest who, in his love affair with God, was very much the down-trodden partner.

'I've got to go,' he said. 'Can you understand, accept that I don't want to camouflage in their money.'

'Camouflage,' said Lucy, panicking. 'The lizard's gone. It was near the leg of the chair. Don't move,' she said to the priest, 'you might tread on it.'

'We'll have to comb the carpet systematically,' said Titus. 'The door's closed. We can each start in a different corner.'

'This reminds me of something,' said Lucy. 'In reverse.'

'What?' asked the priest, guiltily, on all fours. He felt responsible for the metaphysical elaborations which led to the creature's disappearance. 'I'll start here.'

'It's odd, but this suggests Tasmania to me,' said Lucy, 'of combing through Tasmania for the aborigines. Of those extremely thorough grid lines they drew to ensure extermination.'

'You mean the English?' asked Titus.

'Is that how you live with it?' said Lucy. 'We'll have to inch our way slowly. I'm terrified of squashing it.'

'I had a dog which got run over in Adelaide,' said Titus.

'We must save our dragon,' said Lucy, 'from becoming a pet. We'll give him his freedom.'

'It's this damn carpet,' said the priest. 'It's so three-dimensional. And the room's bloody hot too. If we leave it here, it'll grow back into a dinosaur.'

'Don't worry,' said Titus, relieved, 'I've found it. Right under the light.'

'That's good,' said the priest, 'because I really must be going.'

He left quickly, taking long embarrassed strides as if he still felt obliged to tread carefully.

Lucy and Titus, alone in the room, with a shoebox tight and secure in one corner, laughed.

'He's extraordinary,' said Lucy. 'I can just imagine him trying to negotiate for that money.'

'I don't know how he managed to get fifty per cent out of those businessmen,' said Titus. 'It must have been his ideas which beat them down. But old Father Kelleher would have got the lot in one hit.'

'He reminds me of myself a few years back,' said Lucy.

Titus was amused by this. She was not yet twenty-three, with the spiritual precocity of a young boy not long initiated.

'You remind me of myself a few years back,' he said affectionately, placing his hands on her shoulders.

'What were you like a few years back?' she asked, feeling an almost painful curiosity. 'What were you like?' she repeated.

'I wanted to be a healer in my tribe,' he said. 'I kept a bag of quartz crystals, my mother's turinga, some lizard blood, powdered bone, and a full set of my first dog's teeth.'

'I read about magic too when I was young,' she said. 'I had the saints. When the devil changed his shape into a rabid dog the saints had the skill to know it was the devil, and they'd say "away with thee Satan to thy inferno drear", and Satan would change back into himself, looking even more hideous than when he was a rabid dog.'

'Yes,' he said, 'I remember them from school. But they never punished anyone, did they? I always thought that disappointing.'

'God punishes.'

'What use were the saints then?' asked Titus.

'They were examples of model human behaviour.'

'You mean ancestors,' he said. 'They were like ancestors without authority. What did you like about them?'

'They were punished without deserving to be.'

'I know lots of saints then,' laughed Titus. 'There was one Loridja man whose wife killed him for sleeping with his other wife. She thought the other woman was dead when she wasn't. The other woman had gone into a strange sort of coma that looked like death, and the Loridja man kept her near him and slept with her, because it had happened before. But nobody believed him, and they accused him of violating the dead. When she eventually came out of her sleep, her husband was killed, and she was about to be burned.'

'Have you ever used magic?' asked Lucy, worried by his story.

'Yes, of course,' he said, 'everyone uses it. Renkaraka once asked me to pray over a pearl shell because he used to believe that my magic was the strongest in the tribe.

'He wanted a woman who wasn't interested in him. It was a beautiful shell; it had to be, with soft curves, delightful indentations. We set to praying over it, both of us. I rubbed it hard for several hours to give it a strong electric charge. It wasn't easy, it took all my strength. When we had finished we hung it over a digging stick. I remember how beautiful it looked in the late hour of the afternoon, slung, half open to face the setting sun.

'It had to stay there until night. And Renkaraka, when it was dark (I could feel his hands burning), took the shell and put it round his neck.

'When the men came out to dance in front of the women for a special corroboree, he was there with his heavy piece of shell, swinging from side to side.

'He began to dance before everyone else. I had to tell him not to wear the magic out with all his excitement. But the shell was alive with dance. When the women came out, they were entranced. All of them. I could see their eyes fixed on Renkaraka, and nobody else. As if his shell cup would hold all their delights. Communal desire is like separate branches thrown onto the one fire. And I was ready with the other men.

'The dance grew faster. The friction of skin increased as everyone awaited the lightning flash of choice. The line of electrons, floating from the pearl shell through the air, to rest on one woman, to separate out the one he desired. To deepen the division, to enter, push upon push of desire, until she was refreshed by his rainmaking, as the desert welcomes ephemeral bliss and sends flowers.'

'It's like a prince and princess starting a ball,' said Lucy, foolishly. Embarrassed by the beauty of his description, she was unable to look at him.

'There were others who started the dance on different occasions.'

'Did you?' asked Lucy, knowing she would hear the truth.

'No,' he said calmly. 'No.'

'Why don't we take the lizard back to the desert,' said Lucy, relieved, 'and give it its freedom? Where did you find it?'

'I've begun a picture of you,' said Titus. 'I haven't sung over it, or used any magic. You must refuse me before I can use magic.'

'But I don't want to refuse you,' she said.

'Good,' he said, taking her hand. 'Then we will have much more time together, as we have had already in dreams.'

It was true. Lucy had desired him from the time she had begun dreaming of him. From the time she had detected regard creeping in like a sleepy child, cherub-fisted and swallowing air.

He had been in her thoughts constantly, propping up her experience with meaning, giving greater clarity to her observations. She believed they would grow together, so they could consume and enjoy their passion in the stretch of years ahead. Time would be a full-grown angel for them, with a wingful of blessings. It would scatter the seconds benevolently, and they would fall like seeds onto the earth to grow.

'But I'm afraid I'm different from you,' she said. 'Perhaps you'll find me too different.'

'No you're not,' he said confidently. 'You are the rainbow and I'm the snake. They change constantly, one into the other. In my tribe a person gives his beloved a piece of feathered string. The string is the snake. The feather carries it into the sky to make a link with the gods. It becomes a contract, and the contract is the rainbow.'

'I understand,' said Lucy.

'I thought a piece of animal hair with feathers might look primitive to you,' he said, full of humility and anxious to give her his gift.

'No,' she denied emphatically, 'not when there is meaning behind it.'

'I have made something a little different,' he said. 'I decided to make it three weeks ago.'

He went into his room and brought out a necklace, exquisite in its detail. Threaded onto silk were clumps of tiny pearls and red-painted berries, separated by delicate feathers.

'My mother gave me the pearls,' he said. 'They were given to her by the lady she used to do ironing for.'

'It must have taken you all your time to make this,' said Lucy.

'Three weeks,' he repeated. 'I couldn't get to class.'

'I will have to find something for you,' she said, too affected to speak any further.

There was a time of quietness as they lay side by side on the floor. The air was still, and peace was above them, a hovering bird, fanning their anticipation.

'But before we do anything,' she said, unsteadily, 'we must give our lizard its freedom.'

10

It was almost the end of first term, and Lucy's class, having struggled through a D. H. Lawrence short story, felt itself a class with a cause. Their teacher and coon lover had no right to be telling about men and women together.

Sometimes, when their eyes had met, Mr Harrison had wanted to punch Titus for looking at Lucy, punch him until his eyes bulged white on their stalks. Making up to authority. Digging out the white witchetty-grub woman as it pleased him. A black stick man with a hideous pink tongue, licking up every word she said as if he could understand all the rubbish about flowers and the working classes.

There would have to be some sort of delegation to the college to represent their dissatisfaction. Mrs White had nominated him, and Mr Harrison, unused to responsibility, accepted the opportunity with relish. He would tip that senile piece of incompetence out of his caravan. The college administration, for the first time in its life, would have to listen to the voice of the people.

'Mr Robbins,' he said, glancing sideways at his grandson, 'I have not come to quibble. After major consideration of the matter at hand, I have not come to quibble.'

'I know exactly how you feel,' said Mr Robbins, looking into Mr Harrison's startled eyes. 'We have no choice, I agree. We have no choice but not to quibble. If only we were a university, we could offer more choice.'

'I don't want a university,' said Mr Harrison angrily.

'Just a little more choice,' agreed Mr Robbins sympathetically.

'We have no choice,' repeated Mr Harrison automatically. He was totally confused.

'Nor has my grandson,' said Mr Robbins. 'We have tried to get him interested in different foods, but he goes back to the same old things.'

'I know,' said Mr Harrison, suddenly remembering. 'We have no choice but to complain.'

'Of course you don't,' said Mr Robbins. 'I'm always encouraging people to complain. How else will we get things done? I would like to see those Canberra people come up and see the conditions we work under. It seems, you know, Mr Harrison, that I'm going to get my prestige house, which does indeed prove the efficacy of complaining. Sometimes I think we should offer courses in complaining, and call them communications diplomas. There are special skills required for everything, you know.'

'I'm sorry,' said Mr Harrison, 'I think you should be teaching people how to read and write.'

'Yes I quite agree,' said Mr Robbins, his good-natured irrelevance having the soothing effect of sucking on marshmallow. 'Communication is what we need, and how else but in reading and writing. You know I heard this funny story the other day from my doctor. A man came in to him asking if he could be fitted out with a pair of glasses. He said, "Doctor, I've never been to school, so I'll need me a pair of glasses so I can read." '

Mr Harrison gave a half laugh and quickly tried to remember if any of his acquaintances had recently gone to get glasses.

'I've come to complain about one of your teachers,' he said. 'A Miss Stapleton in the first instance.'

'Not Lucy,' said Mr Robbins, completely taken aback. 'Her qualifications are excellent. We are extremely lucky to have her.'

'She's very young,' said Mr Harrison, feeling guilty for the first time.

'But everyone who comes here is young,' said Mr Robbins, 'except me. Older people get settled in the capital cities. And if it weren't for the fact that I'm a gypsy at heart, I wouldn't be here either.'

'It's just that they send them up young from the south, with their D. H. Lawrence and their communism.'

'My goodness,' said Mr Robbins, snatching a biscuit from his grandson before it fell on the floor. 'I didn't realise that D. H. Lawrence was a communist. I suppose that anyone who comes from a coal mine has to be. I'll suggest to her that she change the syllabus. I'm sure P. G. Wodehouse wasn't one.'

'And there's an aborigine in the class.'

'Titus, you mean?' asked Mr Robbins. 'Titus Hayes.'

'Yes. He hasn't been able to fit in. He's taken it upon himself to disrupt the class with politics, and discrimination, and his own ideas about literature.'

'But surely you all have different ideas.'

'I've got me work cut out following what she's saying with her adjectives. She talks direct to the black and he pretends he understands everything. It's like the Imperial New Clothes. She gabbles on, he pretends she's talking sense, and the rest of us feel cheated. I didn't come to English class to feel like that. I get enough of that in me job, and I've had it up to here.'

Mr Harrison stood up to put his weight behind his statement. The pupils of his eyes had that rapidity associated with night drivers and those who, over long distances, have to stay awake.

'I'm always putting meself out,' he said, 'for everyone else. But she won't even give us decent spelling. It's a slap in the face. And there are them in the town who won't put up with a slap in the face from an upstart telling us to expend our minds when she's making up to a black. There's not much argument about what's going on between them, and our minds are expending all right. But it's mainly the spelling I want, and I have been delegated to get it.'

'I will have to investigate this, Mr Harrison. Are you prepared to have me investigate it?'

'Yes,' he said, 'investigate all you like, but we want a new teacher.'

'Have you got any idea how long it takes to get somebody up here?' asked Mr Robbins. 'We will probably just have to close the course altogether.'

'I don't care what you do.'

'I'll have to look into it,' said Mr Robbins. 'I'll need at least another term to sort things out.'

'Do what you like,' said Mr Harrison, speaking with the brevity of victory.

As soon as he had left, Mr Robbins addressed his grandson in the rambling relaxed way he addressed everyone. He put a handkerchief to the boy's nose.

'You can blow now that that man's gone. He's gone. Look. Nobody. Give me your sleeve. Now we'll just tuck it away. Poor Lucy. My goodness, how many handkerchieves have you got stuffed up there? I can't believe she would like D. H. Lawrence, not at her age. So young and innocent, she reminds me of myself when I first went to work and there were pictures of those naked women everywhere.

'There were a lot then like Mr Harrison. They asked me to the pub once. When I said I had to be home for dinner, one of them excreted onto a plate and said there was no need to go home. Times were rough during the Depression. People in jobs were expected to keep together when they didn't like one another.

'Poor Lucy. She's not very old. And you like her, don't you Damian? She brought you in some biscuits the other day. They weren't the kind the doctor would like you to have. I'm sick of doctors.

'And Titus, he's a bright young man. I don't blame them for courting each other. If they could just gain some sort of advantage, an edge on the others in the class. What if I gave them my prestige house? Not for good you understand, Damian, but on loan. I'm sure they'd love it. They would let you use your sandpit there. It will be magnificent when I finish it.

'A prestige house, after all, will do what it says it will do. It will confer prestige. As things stand at the moment I don't need prestige. If I make a sand mountain to start off with, it will take you a while to work your way down. I have no doubt you will want to excavate as soon as possible. And your arms are getting stronger all the time.

'They will gain more status in the community if they are in a good house. Doesn't everyone?'

Mr Robbins decided forthwith that Lucy's job would be saved if he intervened. He would have to move out the few things he had moved in. Of course if his wife had still been alive, then it might have been a different question. But she wasn't, and he had become a gypsy at heart.

Matthew, back from the bush for five days was like Mr Robbins, eager for them to move out. He had sensed a deepening division. Titus and Lucy were spending all their time together. There were no more discussions as before. The two had become, if he were honest, lazy and careless of other people. He respected his brother, but not in the new light-headed partnership he had formed.

'I really think you should accept his offer,' said Matthew.

'It would be unlucky to refuse such generosity. I think there are only five other people in town with a prestige house. The director of our medical unit put in for one, but he's been waiting over a year.'

'Is this supposed to be some sort of exile?' said Titus.
'You know that Esther can look after herself.'
'She's getting old now,' said Titus. 'What if there's another fight like the last one, the last big one she had?'
'I'll be in town over the next few months,' said Matthew more gently than before. 'After that, perhaps you can move back in.'
'With or without Lucy?' asked Titus.
'Why should it come to that?'
'Because you're saying it will soon be over,' said Titus angrily. 'You're putting me down, and like a white man you're putting time limits on everything.'
'It seems odd to me,' said Matthew, 'that you didn't ask my permission to have her here when I first got back from Papunya. It's a simple courtesy.'
'You didn't ask my permission when she first arrived.'
'She was only here for a short stay.'
'You weren't eager to put time limits on things then though,' said Titus.
'I'm not throwing you out, but seeing as though another house has been offered.'
'It's so disappointing,' said Titus. 'I expected you to rise above your jealousy. I was hoping that being out bush might restore your perspective. Instead it has made you petty.'

They had had fights before as boys, but this was the first where the stakes were permanent division, mortality.

'I've had plenty of time to think,' said Matthew, some bitterness in his voice. 'I brought Lucy into the house on trust. You didn't question how much I cared for her.'
'I knew she didn't care for you,' Titus said indignantly. 'That was why I was unfriendly to her in the beginning.'
'Well I don't care for her all that much,' said Matthew, dishonestly.
'If you need more time,' said Titus, 'then be honest

about it. Don't cut me off. I would like the option of coming back.'

They were interrupted by Lucy. Guilt had drawn her awkwardly to the moment, forcing it out into the open before its time.

'Matthew and I have just come to an agreement,' said Titus, 'to leave my paintings here.'

'That's very good of you, Matthew,' she said, 'and thank you for allowing me to stay all this time.'

'It's a matter of course,' said Titus quickly, before Matthew had had time to reply, 'for brothers in the Aranda to share their house with relatives, and the friends of a relative.'

'Well, tradition or not,' said Lucy, 'I'm extremely grateful.'

It was not that Matthew really wanted Lucy. Not any more. She had shown no inclination towards him. But he feared the triangle. If they'd been living in the tribe, no one pattern could have been imposed. Yet he couldn't go back to that life.

Now he was an adult. He had to speak of people, not tribes. He had to help 'his people'. He was expected to be an individual, different, and the multitude of different tribes, the same. That was the logic of his new situation, It was beginning to turn him inside out.

He had studied many years to be white, and he'd been slapped in the face for his trouble. It was, undoubtedly, a minor admonition that Lucy and Titus had fallen in love. He had not cared for her as much as his brother had. But there was a certain perversity in seeing the two people he most respected take such a logical course. In spite of the scale, the distance involved, it was white man's geometry. He left the room in disgust, realising he would find little comfort in his textbooks, should he choose to read them, with their diagrammatic promises of universal anatomy.

11

'I don't expect you to get the garden started. It won't be an easy job,' said Mr Robbins. 'It'll have to be back-hoed first, and we'll need more sand for the sandpit.'

'Are you sure you don't mind all this?' asked Lucy, wanting to be more grateful for the monstrosity in double brick set into the hard clay of outback soil.

'And you'd have to get runners from somewhere,' he said. 'It's no use without runners.'

'You mean grass seeds?' asked Lucy.

'No,' he said, 'you can forget seeds. I couldn't even get a small garden to start around my caravan when I used seeds. You have to get runners with root systems on them. The longer the better.'

'Can you buy them?'

'No,' he said, 'I'll have to steal some from the college without the caretaker knowing. You see he's always complaining about people who take runners. What a splendid house this is. Would any government in the world spend so much money? It shouldn't be difficult to encourage academics up here, not with these facilities.'

In the Lucky Jim world of the older man, Alice Springs needed only ivy and cloisters to be complete. Ivy was adaptable. It could be grown even in the desert. Then Ian Carmichaels would come, frogs in pockets, fumbling for handkerchieves, wiping the sweat off their faces in gratitude at being given the opportunity to ride bicycles in the heat.

Lucy wanted to laugh at the disarray of images in her

mind. The men in black robes, with Ealing faces drying to parchment in the heat, the townspeople unsympathetic to their clumsiness. In the sun, when the bitumen stuck to shoes, the very last bicycle would soften under their weight. All would deride the wobbly distinctions these professors made, in life, on paper, when others had to work for a living.

'Do you really think a university is a possibility?' asked Lucy, looking at a distance of white linoleum floor reminding her of public hospitals.

'It's something I've decided to devote my last years to achieving.'

'It certainly is a grand ambition,' said Lucy. 'But I think you'll have to attract students. I don't think there'd be any in my class who'd be interested.'

'Have you heard about poor Mr Harrison?' asked the principal. 'He's going to lose his job. His work is contracted from the government. But they're going to reallocate his job to government employees, to amalgamate with their transport division.'

'What did he say about my moving into this house?' asked Lucy, trying to feel sympathetic.

'He said something under his breath about the government and how kind it was.'

'How kind?' asked Lucy. 'Or its kind? Anyway it doesn't matter. At least he'll drop out of the class. I don't know why he hasn't dropped out already.'

'That lovely Mrs White brought me some delicious pickles last week.'

'He hasn't talked for such a long time,' continued Lucy. 'And his skin looks red and prickly, as if he has an allergy.'

'Do you think so?' said the frail Robbins. 'He looks very healthy to me. A burly fellow, positively burly, as is the wont of truck drivers.'

'He spends most of his time looking sullenly at the

board,' said Lucy, 'and occasionally sending out little cactus prickles of spite to Titus.'

'Give him a good laugh,' said Mr Robbins, who had never been able to make his grandson smile.

'He seems to suck his face inwards somehow,' said Lucy. 'It's an implosion effect, going into a more general vacuum of discontent. Perhaps I should resign.'

'Resign?' said Mr Robbins in horror. 'One of the few qualified people we've been able to attract. You, my dear, will be the foundation stone of our splendid new university. You will constitute the vanguard of the English Studies Department. You'll be the ambassadorial jewel we'll show to the great cities of this country to encourage young hopefuls with their initials hot from the printing press.'

I'm very grateful to be part of it all,' said Lucy. The Grand Vizier was intent upon seducing her with his magic. 'I would feel better if you sat down.'

Lucy invited him towards the desolate vinyl community of chairs which sat like Stonehenge on the wide plain of linoleum floor.

'They're very comfortable these chairs,' said Mr Robbins. 'I do hope my grandson likes his sandpit. Sand is the colour of biscuit and that alone is a considerable factor. I suppose I'll have to get Council permission first.'

'To build a sandpit?' laughed Lucy, thinking of the comments Father Scarf might make. 'Be careful they don't mix cement in while you're not looking.'

He didn't understand this last remark, attributing it to the wit of the academic which is often removed from life.

'Anyway,' he said, 'when you see Mrs White, tell her I have an orange tree which, if she wants to make marmalade, she is welcome to plunder. Give my regards to Titus. I think Congress want to see him about something.'

After a brief inspection of the sandpit in the back yard,

Mr Robbins left. The house seemed lonelier without him. Lonely and modern with a plethora of appliances soliciting from each dull room corner. Fridge, washing machine, dryer, air-conditioner, can-o-mat, dish washer, waste disposal. They posed in corners drab white or grey. If only her mother could see it. She would be pleased that her daughter had a washing machine, a refrigerator which made no noise.

Alas, this frozen paradise would be ruined by the entrance of Othello, her daughter's paramour, suffocating his passion into a pillow. There was poor Lucy, throat full of goose-down. 'Why,' her mother might ask herself, 'did Stapletons take risks.' She had trained her daughter to be conservative. Now, just as a lovely home was achieved, she threw herself into the arms of a nomad. Othello had not known his own strength. A bone-crushing savage when his blood was high. And her poor foolish daughter would be bound to ask him questions in bed, which was not the time.

Adelaide had been threatening to visit. This seemed to Lucy a most inadvisable move. There had been problems in the town, small enough, but the atmosphere was hostile. The reproving voice of her friend rang in her ears. 'Don't expect it to work. Enjoy it while you can. There's a high incidence of syphilis amongst the aborigines. Wasting yourself. Your mother lonely.'

Adelaide would throw them all up with the energy of a prospector, welcoming adverse conditions in the hope of later success. Lucy could not allow her to come such a distance and fail. It would be better she didn't come at all.

Memories she had pushed to the back of her drawer like stained linen, came back to her in these new sterile surroundings. She recalled the lead-light windows of her house in Haberfield. The marble fireplaces that let in the rain. Darkness and walnut veneer. Neighbours with eyes adapted for darkness and the thickness of curtains. Dark interiors which were so different from the treeless, flat expanse of light outside. So much light, thought Lucy, could not disinfect the staleness within.

She remembered the feeling of dread in the suburb. How it filled the air with a sense of hiding out. The fear that someone would cross a verandah, the moat of rotting wood to apprehend. It was a fierce suburb, where the aged had once been young.

Ironically, she had expected the same dingy palms that graced Haberfield to be present in this desert oasis. But there were few.

Lucy felt a brief desire to escape this new rectangle of stage, where necks craned for a view of woman degraded, where eyes looked through peep holes opened by obliging can-o-mats or by the twin lasers of Mr Harrison's contempt. She wondered if Titus would feel the same way. Men rarely felt at risk from the anonymous voyeur. Although perhaps it was different in aboriginal society. From what she had heard, most of the law prohibited women from looking at men, especially at times of male vulnerability.

It was with relief she noticed Titus and Father Scarf walking through the front gate.

'I'm so glad you're here,' she said. 'Welcome to the academic breeding ground.'

She was interrupted by Father Scarf who noticed a big black-pink bruise on her arm.

'It's come up all right,' said Titus sorrowfully. 'Lucy got into a fight with my relatives last week. She took my mother's side when Aunty Eunice jumped the fence.'

'I don't feel too bad now,' said Lucy, thinking back to when Mrs Hayes had taken off her shirt to fight. Dust, dogs, breasts, muscle and the high-pitched abuse of warriors. However, it had been, as these things went, a minor skirmish, as Lucy had kept all bottles and implements at a discreet distance.

'I dislike my mother fighting,' said Titus sympathetically. 'And I hope Lucy doesn't interfere again.'

'Eunice's always been jealous of your mother,' said Lucy, 'for having had a white husband. She's a stupid drunk of a woman.'

'One day my mother's going to lose a fight,' said Titus, 'and I'll have a murder on my conscience.'

'A payback you mean?' asked Father Scarf.

'No,' said Titus bitterly, 'that's the problem. I won't be able to take practical revenge, so I'll have her death on my conscience.'

'But that won't matter to your mother, will it?' said the priest. 'You can't bring her back to life.'

'I can guarantee her spirit will rest,' he said. 'Otherwise she'll have to avenge the person herself, and that's more difficult to do when you're dead. The responsibility should and does rest with the living.'

'But you're a Christian,' said the priest. 'A Catholic.'

'Yes,' said Titus, looking for the first time at the desolation that was the house.

'Is that why you're so protective of her?' asked Lucy, feeling now that she understood him better. She had seen that Esther was still able to look after herself, but if she did get killed in a fight, Titus wouldn't be able to pay her murderer back.

'That's the way it should be,' said the priest, stroking his beard anxiously.

'That's the way it has to be,' said Titus.

'Then it is your supreme duty to keep your mother out of fights,' said the priest. 'That way you will have a clear conscience.'

'What if she believes someone wants to kill her by sorcery?' asked Titus. 'It's not as simple as you think.'

'You don't believe in that kind of superstition?' asked the priest.

'Some of it,' said Titus. 'One can't believe everything.'

'Don't worry,' said Lucy. 'I can't imagine your mother dying from other than natural causes.'

'I'm not worried, I'm depressed,' he said, looking at Lucy. 'I've got to spend a fair bit of time out bush. Aboriginal Legal Aid needs witnesses for the murder trial coming up. They'll be day trips mostly and you'll be able to come along. But I won't be able to stay tonight.'

It filled Lucy with despair to think of spending her first night in the new subdivision alone. The practicalities of life were already coming between them. They had so little time together. She resolved to write to Adelaide immediately to discourage her visit.

'I've got to find reliable witnesses,' he said, 'and that's not easy to do. They'll tell me what they think I want to hear. We all do that of course. But they misconstrue what is expected.'

'And they won't hide information either,' said Father Scarf, 'which misdirects the course of justice because law is geared up to detect the liar.'

'Yes,' agreed Lucy, distractedly. She felt it was equally difficult to hide her disappointment at Titus going away.

Father Scarf, realising she was depressed, attempted to be cheerful.

'Lucy will have the opportunity to meet many murderers up here,' he said. 'That alone will make her trip worthwhile. What could be more romantic than acquiring a black lover with an entourage of murderers.'

'You're right,' smiled Lucy. 'You should marry us and take the romance out of it. A married woman with an entourage of murderers doesn't sound quite so impressive. As a member of the Church you have an obligation to demoralise.'

'Yes,' he smiled thoughtfully, 'morals and morays are slippery eels. I wonder why the Church has anything to do with them. I prefer the concept of a natural law where life above all other things is respected.'

'I would like to marry you,' said Titus softly to Lucy, 'in spite of the entourage of murderers.'

They talked the length of the afternoon. It was dark when they left, and Lucy felt lonelier and more isolated than before. She walked outside and stood on the clay next to a small pile of building debris. The night was hot. Heat radiated from the bricks. Upright and alone, she stared at the immaculately curbed and guttered road. In the distance were the ranges, their ribs standing like the backbone of an old horse against a new-moon light, and the stars dangled over the ancient country, dangled like quicksilver spurs in the blackness.

12

Alice Springs

Dear Adelaide,

I don't know how to start a letter that is going to be discouraging. I could apologise for the length of time I haven't written, then ask you not to come up as intended. A rude double-or-nothing rebuff. Can I therefore explain the circumstances which have necessitated this rudeness, and allow you to judge the timing of your visit?

I have fallen in love with the half-caste Titus whom I have mentioned before. However my happiness has been complicated by a variety of problems. As you know I have never claimed to love anybody before. I find it hard to believe I can be loved in return. It's the most wonderful form of desert barter. In the desert one gets one's desserts. It is right that only one small snake should separate the words. In truth I have got much more than I deserve, and so has he, which is what makes love special, and me, now, unable to sleep.

So I'm writing to let you know how I feel, and how certain sections of the community are jealous. Where shall I begin? There's Mr Harrison who's about to lose his job. He believes it will be saved (by the skin of his teeth) because he's white, and his teeth are false. He's been lobbying to have me removed from my job at the college. He would tell you, if he had the chance, that the pulp of the white woman is illicit for the black digging stick. There are many obscenities I read in his eyes.

There is, as you can imagine, a lot of tension when we walk together in the town, and absolutely no question of Titus putting his arm around me, or even touching me in public. It's odd being at the town's mercy.

I can't understand the prejudice. So many of the townspeople are public servants who seem to have acquired their hatred with unnatural quickness. In their bureaucratic world there should be slowness, checks within the system. But this is generally not the case. ghey come here on transfer, and within the year are talking like locals.

Of course there are many people in the town who are reasonable. You know Matthew; although he seems to be turning a little strange. And there's Father Scarf who's even more idealistic than I used to be. I'm not so now. I have become stingy with my time, my privacy with Titus. I have the greed of the pauper who is suddenly made rich. Je suis maintenant (actuellement) le nouveau amour. But I have such a dread they will shake me out of my happiness, like a ripe apple out of a tree.

Mr Robbins, in his kindness, on his blindness, has offered me the use of his prestige house. This is a great honour. And there is a mound of sand at the back of the house awaiting the finishing touches. He's building a sandpit for his grandson.

Why does the man have to be such an angel? He makes me feel uneasy. Angels, you know, are only supposed to make short visits before they disappear. Nevertheless I don't want to give you the wrong impression. He is a dear man and very much in contrast to others in the town.

I'm sorry. I haven't explained why he has given me the house. He has given it to me to allay suspicion about my character and my credentials as a teacher. In the future he hopes to establish a university with me as head of the English Department. Fanciful you think, for a town this size. True. And over Mr Harrison's unemployed body.

Before I describe a recent incident to you, let me say I will be spending a lot more time out bush, now that a trial is pending, and one of the Aranda is facing a murder charge. A man was killed by a spear a few days ago. According to Titus's information, the spear went too close to the heart. It had only been intended to wound. But Renkamara's relatives tripped while they threw the spear. Two of them had been trying to throw it at once. They'd been drinking. It is a terrible shame that alcohol has come to his people. It makes them no better than blunt stones that white men can use to sharpen their own knives against.

Anyway it concerns the time that Titus and I went out to dinner in one of the motel restaurants. You can imagine the sort of place – mood and muzak, fake stardust, people with exaggerated table manners leaning over fat candles, all a-splutter and a-flicker for the night out. Overcooked sirloin, potatoes covered in shreds of tinfoil. Sweet wine everywhere, and the women down one end of the table.

I can hear the men now, discussing their matters of importance. Faces full. Words oozing out of their mouths as if coming from a sausage machine, the long drawl of accent, covered with the intestine of gut response. 'Why doesn't he wake up to himself. You can't operate without a light aircraft these days. I mean you may as well be a boong as think like that. Mind you, the coons don't have it too bad these days with their fucking excuse my French health service, their legal aid and their unemployment benefits. It's more than we get. They can afford to eat in restaurants, some of them.'

They then, as you can imagine, proceeded to make a tableau of Titus and me. At first we ignored it, but their voices were extremely loud. Later they were joined by a man who had once served me cappuccino.

In these dire surroundings, Titus looked more beautiful

than ever to me. The strong, high bones of his cheeks, a grace of move-ment which for a time made me feel clumsy, and sad for the dull canine eagerness of my race.

Matthew was supposed to meet us at the restaurant, as it had been his idea to have dinner together in order to settle our differences. (There are some problems. I don't think they're too serious.) Anyway, he didn't turn up, which together with the comments from our neighbours, ruined the night.

But Titus, it makes me happy to think about him, was doing his best to make me feel better. He was telling me of animals and their strange habits, trying to excuse the people at the other table for my sake.

Just when we had decided to leave, our patience having been well and truly tested, our neighbours began to make signs of departure. One of them downed a Tia Maria, others allowed napkins to slip to the floor; handbags were moved, people bacame couples, half up, half down and cantan-kerous. Only the cappucino man appeared organised. He stood alone, waiting for the others to leave the table.

When they had left he came calmly over to our table. He rolled his jaw, and with some worked-up spit in his mouth, deposited it into Titus's soup. The spittle lay, like stained egg white, floating on top. It was obvious that what had sobered him (he'd arrived drunk) was his hatred for us. So we left the restaurant immediately. Titus then was too shocked to do or say anything. Since the event he's been talking of revenge.

It's all rather difficult. When I left school I believed that the bullies were buried, that Suzie and Mavis would find themselves husbands, docile and drear, and all would be well.

But it now seems clearer than ever that there will always be foes who dislike the way I part my hair, the colour of my dress, the skin colour of my beloved. My enemies are springing from Cadmus's teeth, worthier and more plentiful than ever. The more I scratch this discomfort, the itchier it gets. The only problem is diagnosis. The cappuccino man had looked so quiet, had been the least boisterous of all.

I don't miss Sydney, only you and my mother. My mind turns to Grandfather's too, a row of shabby pines, a rainwater tank, fruit trees, fly-screen doors, cattle dogs, all the unfulfilled dreams of the grazier on the edge of something hard. I think of a loose edge of sandstone cliff facing the Pacific. But in reverse. It will, I suspect, erode away. It will all erode away. How much better I would feel if there were volcanos in this country.

They have begun to cut the cedar trees. The shops look odd, as there is no light and shade to give the illusion of depth. The tree trunks are like the torsos of tourists soon to leave the town. Here, there and everywhere, they trail blood from their crosses.

There will soon be nothing left. I don't mind. It's not a pretty town. It's drab and modern and full of old ladies who have left the graves of their husbands to tour Australia. They take their last big look at the continent before they croak. The red heart, attacks. You can see them climbing up The Rock, taking long trips on rough roads, photos of piccaninnies, their zippered bags only a little smaller than the airline coffin.

'Excuse I,' they ask me, taking a good look at Titus 'could you tell me where the School of the Air is situated?' And when I tell them that it's quite a distance, they look back at me as if the distance were my fault, that I am responsible for their lives full of mistakes they would have done 'all over again, given the chance'. I watch them in their flatties and sunhats, bent into the heat as if it were a cyclone. Perhaps I should feel sorry for these oppressed, as they surely are. But I find, if I'm honest with myself, that I'm ruthlessly selective, and that these people are victims of old age, which is not selective.

Please, if you think Titus is like Matthew, you're wrong, very wrong. Matthew is white, no different from me. White and earnest. He knows very little about the ways of his people, yet is full of sympathy for the theory of it all, for himself as a half-caste.

Titus is intelligent. He is proud, but he accepts that he must from time to time mend wounds with a zig-zag stitch. He is conscious of the way we use sex, religion, nationality to find fault with the world, and yet he sees that it is a world which should be faulted. He has a keen sense of beauty. It is this which separates him most from Matthew.

Lately Matthew has become demoralised. He feels he has not received enough status for becoming a doctor. There are too many diverse tribes for him to deal with, some of them he cannot relate to.

I'm missing Titus terribly tonight. He is wonderful, passionate, worthy of love and respect. You will have the chance to meet him when things settle down, when the town gets tired of peddling us as pornography. I know you will like him. He is the truest part of self and country to me.

I can say no more. I am miserable and desperate for him. Hold off your visit until I'm a saner Lucy. The least I can do (you think) is to offer you a saner Lucy.

                                                Your Dear Friend

13

'I don't want to be too close to a water hole,' said Titus. 'This way no one will disturb us.'

They had set up camp in one of the many dry watercourses that wound through the valleys and low parts of the country. Scattered in the sandy river bed were jerry cans holding their water supply. River red gums were buried in the quartz of decomposed rock. Their massive trunks wound in strange twists of dove-grey and white. They would give shade in the afternoon, and there was always the smell of moist wood lying dormant under their dry peeling surfaces of bark. In the distance she could see the near-extinct division made by the ranges, between earth and sky.

'This is wonderful country,' said Lucy. It was the end of first term. She stood in the middle of the wide shape of a river, ankle deep in sand. She wondered if it would ever hold water, its bed was so porous. Where might the water go. Perhaps to underground chambers, somewhere cool and fertile where an ancient tribe could perform its secret ceremonies. She remembered reading Peter Pan as a child. He lived inside a vast hollow tree that went underground. Many of the stories she had liked were about people who lived in trees. Animals with human faces who had neat door knockers and welcome mats throughout the forest.

When she was young she had dreamed of living in a tree with a lift inside its trunk, as in the big department stores. The lift would take her up to the tree house or down into cavernous chambers. She preferred the cavernous chambers, where immoral things would happen. Where old men were anxious to touch and try young girls. Each night she added a chamber or decorated what was there with a new piece of paraphernalia.

'There's not much privacy in the desert,' said Titus, seeming to read her thoughts.

'Property and privacy go together,' said Lucy. 'And we haven't got a lot of property with us now.'

'I didn't need privacy when I was young,' said Titus. 'I still don't when I'm with people I like. When I was young I saw everything I wanted. Sex games, hunting games. The old people when they weren't working would tell us stories, touch our genitals perhaps, speculate about the future.'

'When I was young,' said Lucy, 'religion threw its cloak over sex and sadism, not to hide them but to protect and foster them. Nobody taught us about love.'

'I'll get the wood,' he said, kissing her softly on the neck. 'Why did you bring an umbrella?'

'To protect me from the sun,' said Lucy, 'in case we went for food or something.'

'Good idea.' He smiled, looking at its carved handle, its frail ribs and awkward nylon flaps.

'I almost didn't bring it,' she admitted. 'But I was afraid of getting burnt. The nuns used to hit us with them, you see. It makes me laugh how they were able to walk so modestly, hiding the movements of their feet under their habits. Their umbrellas seemed to act as much for propulsion as for shade.'

'You don't think like other whites I've met,' he said, 'even Vivian. Because you treat the past and present as the same. I mean you remember all the little details of your youth, so it doesn't become a romantic refuge for you. Yet you romanticise the future (which is far more sensible) by falling in love with me. You will counteract the bitterness of growing old by love, and the happiness of youth by memory.'

'Are you sure that doesn't amount to paralysis?'

'Yes,' said Titus, 'that's right, it does. It's a way of stunning time, of hitting it over the head.' Titus stretched out in the sun looking pleased with Lucy. The world of the white man had been unable to change her. 'I always thought it ironic,' he continued, 'that the white people who put our people in chains wore heavier ones for themselves. They were the children of convicts, doing time, making time, wasting time. We were less their prisoners because we had disowned the burden of the sentence.'

'But aren't we all prisoners of time?'

'Yes,' he said. 'There's sadness in growing old. But for me it's not the steady countdown it seems to be in white society. Not the tick-tock watchfulness. As far as I'm concerned there's no use making preparations. The animal will bite you when you least expect it. You'll be angry, resentful, so it'll go away, until it makes its final claim. Death is the dog that owns its master. If you are owned you cannot be a prisoner. There's no hope of escape, and there's a greater chance of a working relationship.'

'It's an interesting analogy,' said Lucy. 'But not a convincing one.'

'Isn't it?' He smiled. 'How else will I make you understand. The Aranda don't talk about the meaning of life, they prefer to discuss the misfortunes of their ancestors.'

'You understand so much,' said Lucy awkwardly, thinking that she was not good enough for him.

'I'll get the firewood,' he repeated, embarrassed. 'I want to do everything for you. Tonight we will do everything. And keep the fire going until morning.'

Titus and Lucy stayed up until the hour of condensation drank them into sleep. Dogs slept on either side of them, helping them stay warm in each other's arms.

Lucy woke first. For a while she observed her sleeping partner. A fine line of sleep dust wavered across his eyelids. The sun, over the horizon, was just beginning to warm her back, emphasising the inviting distinction between two worlds, sleeping and waking. She kissed the division in his eyelids, the line of tide which was white, not black.

She sat in the sunlight with a feeling of infinite time. Time to observe Titus, his gentle sleeping motion, the beads of moisture on their tarpaulin, the sounds of jerry can contracting in the coolness of the morning. There was also the smell of damp charcoal, mixed in with fresh smells everywhere. It was too early for the kites to circle.

There was no dawn chorus as she had expected. None of the noise of the south-west, the currawongs winding up like oboes on heavy disc recordings. No squawking rosellas; the memory of their caged and heavy sound was diffracted by the voices of smaller, more delicate birds, zebra finches and the like.

The green patched fur of her family's country seemed a long distance away: its gracefully arched back, full of briars and thistle, patches of lushness where super-phosphate had been capriciously applied. The wild weed which produced delicious honey, Paterson's Curse, would now be in its deep-purple bloom. The enemy of graziers, until the locusts ate it and everything else away.

The desert offered even fewer seductions for grazier and sheep. It was cattle country. Camel country, where at the present time camel food, the poisonous paddy melon, grew in abundance by the side of a track near their camp site. These melons were everywhere, as were the deep-pink flowers planted by the Afghans to help feed their animals.

The Afghans were gone now, except for one old man in the town. Now only the tourists rode the camels, and there were vast numbers of wild dromedaries left to have the time of their lives on the edge of the dune country.

Titus, once the dogs began to move, stirred to wake. The human animal, thought Lucy, took much longer to find a way out of sleep. Birds, dogs and other animals seemed to rush into immediate activity.

'Lucy,' he whispered, stretching his arm towards her, to check she was still present.

She kissed him. The air was warm and still. Little spirals of pleasure ran over them as they embraced.

'I'll relight the fire,' he said.

'The wood's wet,' she said. 'It'll be impossible to start.'

'I buried some last night. The dogs have been sleeping over it.'

'What can we eat for breakfast? I've brought eggs. I couldn't think what else would keep for a long time.'

'Goanna,' he said. 'I thought we'd have goanna. I know you haven't had it before, but it's delicious for breakfast. It tastes a little like fish.'

'It loses some of its flavour when it's cooked?' asked Lucy hopefully.

'Don't worry,' he laughed. 'I've suggested something bland, bland and delicious like avocado. Snake tastes stronger.'

'I'll trust you,' said Lucy. 'I've never hunted for anything, except rabbits and foxes with Grandfather. But you didn't eat them. They were pests, too lowly to eat.'

'I think one shows more respect to the animal one eats,' said Titus, 'or an animal that's useful. You can become business partners.'

'Then the most civilised countries,' said Lucy, digging her toes into the sand of the river bed, 'are those that eat everything, like the Chinese, and the French. But it's important how you treat your partners. You must kill them quickly, cleanly, and with the grace of a *chef de cuisine*. Then you are truly civilised.'

'People often talk about liking to hunt, or disliking to kill,' agreed Titus, selecting a pyramid of choice sticks for the fire. 'For me it's like saying "I like to breathe, I dislike breathing." It's nonsense.'

'Your distinction is a real one,' said Lucy. 'Unfortunately some people are greedy, greedy for money, for blood, for food. Greed is the enemy of life, of breathing if you like. It's the holding of the breath in a tantrum to demand more. It makes a mockery of life, first by denying it and finally by expecting a reward for its anarchy.'

'I can show you how to kill a goanna,' he said, 'quickly and efficiently. I could also show you how to kill a kangaroo. But that would take several years, and you would be too old by the time you got the skill. Anyway, nowadays people use bullets, so anybody can do it.'

'Can Matthew hunt kangaroo?' asked Lucy. 'He would have been in school, I suppose, while you were learning.'

'He can't, no.'

'Did he ever show any curiosity about hunting, the ways of the bush?'

'He was interested in certain things, in initiation for example. He wasn't initiated. But hunting never interested him. Once, I remember, I sent him some kangaroo fat for his football boots. It's very good for leather, it keeps it soft and durable. He got very angry and wrote never to send him parcels of stinking fat again.'

'One of the other boarders must have opened it,' said Lucy. 'The persecution for such an offence would have been terrible.'

'He hated football too,' said Titus thoughtfully. 'I think he wanted to keep his two worlds as separate as possible. The problem was that only he knew what the boundaries were, and when people stepped over them.'

'He's a complicated person,' she said, 'with the weight of two worlds on his back.'

'But that's not a complete answer,' said Titus. 'Most of us have at least two worlds. You had Ireland and Haberfield, I had Adelaide, Alice Springs, the bush. I don't really understand him.'

'Perhaps he's jealous of you,' said Lucy. 'Why wasn't he initiated before he left for school?'

'He would have been frightened,' said Titus, 'like I was.'

'But why didn't your mother make him?' asked Lucy.

'She couldn't get the old men to come for him,' said Titus, his voice full of regret. 'They knew he was going to leave the tribe, so unless he himself had shown more enthusiasm . . .'

'I suppose it's too much,' interrupted Lucy, 'to expect a twelve-year-old boy to be enthusiastic about having his foreskin removed.'

'Yes,' said Titus, moving back from the hot blaze of the fire and pulling his dog away by the hind legs. 'I had a fingernail removed, the underside of my penis split, and was smoked over a fire as well.'

'Did you feel like a man after all that?' smiled Lucy.

'I felt like a baby,' he said, 'and that, if the truth be known, was how they wanted me to feel.'

'But you became a male adult?'

'Before you become an adult,' he said, 'you have to be made a child again. A baby. So I shed blood to represent the afterbirth. The cutting of my foreskin was the cutting of the umbilical cord. When the old men flew fire-sticks over my head, I felt just as helpless as a baby. My mother wailed in the distance with the other women, and I felt more in sympathy with her than ever at the shabby replica of her suffering the ceremony presented.

'Of course it was all essential. And I accepted it in spite of the suffering and those feeble old men who could barely throw a fire-stick. It was only after the bravado had taken place that I began to learn anything. Those old men had all kinds of stories to tell, truths which I can't pass on, even to you. And I remember how I sat back in wonder to listen.'

'You paint such a realistic picture,' said Lucy, 'even a European can understand. I mean, what's the difference between initiation and confirmation, except that women can be confirmed? Confirmation, too, is a renewal of birth. And although I never lost a fingernail through it, I had to kiss a bishop's ring at the confirmation breakfast when I had chicken drumsticks in both hands. He held out his hand for me to take, and both my hands were greasily occupied. In the end I had to show him what I had behind my back. And I didn't in the least feel like an adult Christian.'

'What are you talking about?' laughed Titus. 'Anyway, women are initiated, you know. When they get their periods they go out into the bush with the other women. They are deflowered by a special boomerang. When they come back, they have intercourse with a number of approved partners.'

'Is there any prohibition attached to menstruating? Is it considered dirty?'

'The opposite,' said Titus. 'Blood makes a woman sacred. She must be talked about with respect while she's bleeding. There are many respectful euphemisms which can be used. "She's sitting down on account of her back", "there's something in her foot so she has to sit down" etc.

'When a woman first menstruates they cover her with clay, so she doesn't attract the rainbow snake. The rainbow snake likes the smell of blood. Then they paint a crescent moon on her in white, so that she menstruates monthly and not continually.'

'But there must be some prohibitions,' persisted Lucy.

'The only one that I can think of,' he said, 'relates to intercourse. If a woman has intercourse during her periods, then the man's hair may turn grey. Nobody really believes it of course. But it is agreed that respect and distance are necessary.'

'What do you believe?' asked Lucy.

'That it is perhaps the most sacred cycle of all, and should not be interrupted. Also, my totem is the Rainbow Snake. He would get extremely jealous of the blood.'

'But you've been brought up a Catholic?'

'What pronouncements have they made on the subject?' Titus said, indicating he would like to change topics.

As she retreated into the shade of the tarpaulin, Lucy felt like the proverbial tortoise retreating into its shell. There were so many new, sunny slants on life, she needed protection, reassurance. Moreover, tortoises so often came to grief on a stretch of sand. It was their most vulnerable time.

'You know what I'd like to do,' said Titus enthusiastically. Lucy was pleased he'd forgotten the idea of breakfast. 'I'd like to make you a pair of mud breasts, like young girls get before they are initiated. Or perhaps,' he continued, 'we could both cover ourselves in clay, to look spectacular around the fire tonight.'

'Yes,' agreed Lucy, open to suggestion in the growing heat of morning.

Kites had begun to circle, attracted by the fire, the smell of insects burning in the wood and the sensual world of the two lovers sending them updraughts of delight to support their new and unfurled wings.

'I didn't think Esther would want to come out all this way,' said Lucy, observing from a distance Titus's mother, legs in a spindle, handkerchief covering her head, as she walked towards them.

'You can never tell what she's going to do,' said Titus proudly. Unpredictability, as far as he was concerned, was the mark of her supremacy as a hunter, in the real sense. She was someone who could stalk life successfully, being both reliable and unpredictable. It was a most valuable combination. If she promised to do something she would do it. But she was always careful to guarantee the end rather than the means.

'It's humid, isn't it?' said Esther as she sat down with them under the tarpaulin.

'Yes,' said Titus, curious as to why she would begin by talking about the weather.

'Things are bad in town at the moment,' she said, taking Lucy's hand sympathetically. 'It's very humid.'

'Things are always bad in town,' smiled Lucy.

'You can see the white man breaking out into blisters of sweat,' said Esther. 'And there've been more fights outside the pubs. One hotel has boarded in its windows. You didn't get much of a view anyway, but it's a bad sign.'

'Of what?' asked Titus, searching the sky for a sign of rain.

'That there's a build-up of hatred in the town,' she continued, with the voice of someone who had been through it all before. 'It's as sure as the rain we'll get this afternoon.'

'You're right about the rain,' agreed Titus.

'I think you should both move camp immediately. There'll be flooding in this river before the day's out. There's a bit of a rise to the south. By old Myrtle's grave. Trust her to get buried on the only piece of high ground. It'll stay dry enough, but you won't be able to use it.'

Titus laughed loudly at this, throwing his head back. It was taboo to camp on a burial site, or near the place where someone had died.

'She's been dead ten years,' he said. 'That's long enough in the land of the dead.'

'That might hold for some people,' said Esther seriously, 'but not her. If ever she swept up after camp, or stayed out digging longer, or bathed a sore on a dog's knee, the whole world knew about it. She would send a spirit, quick as a flash, to get rid of you. "What's he ever done for me," she would say and "He's the son of that Esther woman who was after every man in the camp." If I were you I'd find somewhere else to camp.'

'Why did you mention it in the first place, then?' ventured Titus.

'I just wanted to point out what a selfish old bugger she was.'

Titus and Lucy smiled, putting the billy on the fire.

'I'm expecting Matthew,' she continued. A sternness had come into her voice. 'I hope he'll be able to explain better what is happening in town.'

Lucy wondered if the reason for his presence was to be one of reconciliation rather than explanation. Esther had been working steadily towards this, attempting to smooth discontent when it arose.

'We all need Matthew,' she began again, 'at times like this. We need his methods, his surgical methods.'

Silence followed Esther's statement. Lucy felt she could hear the clouds as they made their first tentative movements across the sky. It was a breathing kind of sound, as if the lungs of the desert were ridding themselves of condensation, or some half-voiced asthmatic was questioning her right to be present.

'Everything seems to be swelling out,' said Lucy in the time that followed. 'I suppose it's the humidity. Even this piece of bark here feels softer.'

'Yes,' agreed Titus. 'And you'll hear the calls of courtship made by the birds. When they think it's going to rain they begin their love questing.'

'But don't they have some sort of breeding cycle?' asked Lucy.

'No,' he answered. 'Most of them begin to breed at the first drop of rain. Rain is the semen, if you like, preparing the way for tadpoles, birds, lots of things.'

'I can hear Matthew's car,' said Esther, pleased she had heard before her son, that the humid air had carried the sound more efficiently to her ears.

They listened in silence for several minutes until an engine sound became clearly audible. Matthew's four-wheel drive appeared to be having more difficulty with the terrain than Titus's wide-wheeled Holden.

'I had to let air out of the tyres,' he said, short of breath, anxious. 'I was all right over the claypans, but river beds are a different proposition. I had to let them down to half pressure to get a grip.'

'I'm sorry,' said Titus. The new distance between himself and his brother had imposed politeness on their conversation.

'I've come to say that I think you and Lucy should stay out here for as long as possible. I know what I'm saying is going to sound unfriendly, but I don't mean it in that way.'

There was a new authority in his voice. He had the calmness of someone prepared for disaster, the squirrel with the double ration of nuts, or an adolescent boy with two bank accounts.

'I don't think you should return for a while,' he continued. 'You've got enemies in town.'

'What on earth has happened?' said Titus, surprised and pleased by his brother's gravity. It was a less trivial tone.

'A white woman has been raped and murdered,' he said, looking meaningfully at Esther. She also knew the details.

'I see,' said Titus coolly, reacting no differently from a

white man who learns of an aboriginal death. 'Who?'

'Sandy Morton.'

'But she's a half-caste,' he said indignantly.

'Yes. That's the point,' said Matthew. 'It obviously suits them to classify her as white. She'd been living with a white man along the Todd. I suppose they want to conduct a pre-emptive strike.'

'I imagine they haven't even interviewed her de facto,' said Titus bitterly. 'Not when there are blacks around.'

'It's terrible for her mother,' said Esther. 'They put old Daniel down in Yatala for stealing a car. And now Sandy. She was a delightful little girl. I remember her bringing me a pelican once. She said that she'd taught it to talk.'

'She got onto the grog though,' said Matthew, showing less sympathy for the victims of his own generation, 'which was why she took up with that Noel dross.'

'There's not much chance they'll ask him questions,' said Esther.

'We've got nothing to worry about,' said Lucy, trying to disguise the uncertainty in her voice.

'You have faith in the rule of law?' asked Titus. 'White law?'

'Yes.'

'Then so do I.'

'Nevertheless,' said Matthew. 'I think you should both lie low for a while, like all of us at the moment.'

'If they nab anyone,' said Titus, 'it'll probably be some poor bushman come to town for a binge. He won't understand what's going on, and he'll answer "yes" to all their questions. They'll keep him under arrest to satisfy the people in town that someone's actually being held in custody.'

'Margaret Morton has terrible cataracts growing over her eyes,' said Esther sympathetically. 'When you get a chance, Matthew, look at them for me. She's such a sight in that beach hat she wears.'

'What do you want me to look at,' he smiled, 'the beach hat or the cataracts?'

'Don't be silly,' she said. 'If I don't sound clear it's for a reason.' She paused before resuming. 'A river will turn over a lot of mud before it settles down to do any good, before it sinks into the soil. Give me time. Poor woman. Daniel stole that car to help her relatives.'

'How was her daughter murdered?' asked Lucy.

'A flagon across the throat,' said Matthew. It was a dramatic description for a doctor. 'She bled to death.'

Lucy felt prickly. The tale of Sandy Morton had something of the exemplar in it. As if it had been told to put fear into her heart, to strike one of those cruel parallels she'd been brought up on. She began to feel an unreasonable resentment towards Matthew. She was glad he was leaving. The role of moralist suited him well. But Titus was too preoccupied with the business of reconciliation to acknowledge it.

'Stay longer,' he said to his brother, who had already started his car.

'Let him get back,' said Esther, pleased with the prospect of reconciliation but by no means complacent. Too many terrible things were happening, would happen to her people.

'I don't think Matthew's quite forgiven me for Lucy,' said Titus. 'He had a rather righteous manner, don't you think?'

'At least he's trying,' said Esther sharply. 'Younger brothers learn how to try from the earliest age, and older ones learn not to notice.'

'I know he's trying,' said Titus.

'North-westerly,' said Esther, indicating with her hands the direction the rain would come from. 'You'll have to move your tarpaulin. I've brought you some blankets.'

'There was a bad flood here,' said Titus, 'five years ago.

I remember it. I was camped up the river, and I saw two corpses. White corpses. Accentuated, because the water was brown underneath them. Brown, muscular and kind of interwoven. They kept being thrown up to the surface. Their mouths, particularly their lower jaws, looked like rudders. Loose rudders. They went along with tree roots, trees, car chassis. Sheets of corrugated iron escorted the runaways. It was the stuff of comedy, except their were no drunken relatives to intercept the corpses. No flags, prayers or bunting to help reduce death and stop us seeing our own reflections in glassy corpse eyes.'

'How could they just get washed away?' asked Lucy. 'They must have been able to see the rain coming.'

'There are always people who misjudge, mistime,' he said. 'Timing is one of the most important elements in survival. It relates to instinct though, not the clock.'

'Timing is independent of time,' said Lucy rather automatically.

'If you looked into Sandy Morton's death, for example,' he continued, 'you would probably find that if she'd arrived ten minutes later her assailant's mood might've been different. If she had had the opportunity perhaps she should have tried to rush time on a bit by talking of his intentions. Perhaps then he wouldn't have had time to carry them out before his mood changed.'

'Yes,' said Lucy. 'You've taught me how much time can be expanded and compressed, like the atmosphere. However we'll never know if Sandy Morton was given her opportunity, her saving moment.'

'Perhaps her saving moment came before she left camp,' he said, 'but she decided to leave early because she felt restless and impatient with life. Perhaps she wanted to die.'

'I don't know,' said Lucy. 'It seems to me that we're given a number of possibilities for death; it's the clever ones who are able to use some sort of selection process.'

'Sandy was a highly intelligent girl,' said Esther, taking a stick of tobacco out from the niche of her breasts and breaking a piece off to prepare for chewing. 'She learned how to read faster than her brothers.

'Her mother used to have a picture she painted of a kangaroo. It was a big red, with a face like a happy town dog. Underneath she had two lines in beautiful writing. "The big king brown, slithered past the tall grass with its forked tongue hanging down". Near the huge feet of the kangaroo was the barest glimpse of a snake, blood dripping from its pretty ochre fangs.'

An ominous depression had settled over the small group. It had sprung up from unpromising soil with the promise of rain. It brought with it a sense of profound emptiness waiting to be filled. Waiting for the contents of the wide land to be pumped out before the surgeon rain could take effect. How long would it be before complications developed?

Probably, in due course, she would be expelled as an irritation. Her only concern was that she would be expelled in the company of Titus, the person she loved so dearly.

14

The rain came even more heavily than they expected. By the second day the creek bed was flooded, the trees up to their waists in water. Lightning was mapping the sky for the souls of those to be taken up. Lucy was afraid of lightning. It was heaven's most self-indulgent punishment, with a touch of the pagan about it.

The only sound she could hear was the chorus of frogs. They seemed to be gargling the water in the backs of their throats, relishing the rain, like tourists finding a hot shower in a foreign country.

'Your poor blue lips,' said Titus. 'They've turned into a hideous Namatjira purple. I'm going to take you back to town.'

'I'm all right,' said Lucy, trying not to shiver. 'These woollen blankets are giving off a lot of warmth. I remember the time water got into Grandfather's wool, there was a fire. Wool gives off a lot of warmth when it's wet.'

'You'll end up in hospital,' said Titus, tightening the blanket around her shoulders, insisting she take his.

'It's not safe to go back now,' said Lucy. 'You heard Matthew, your mother. I don't want to go back to that town. It's better out here, even with the rain.'

'That's all very well,' he said. 'If we leave it too much longer we'll be completely cut off. If you get sick, we won't be able to get you into town.'

'I feel completely well,' said Lucy. 'Anyway, you can use sorcery on me if I get sick.'

'You need your own medicine,' he said, disregarding the lightness of her tone. 'Like most of your race you overestimate your adaptability, your strength. It's a great mistake to do that.'

'Well your race goes too far in the other direction,' said Lucy, cold and irritable.

'I'm only thinking of you,' he said. 'I don't have a lot of respect for white medicine, but I think it might be of help to you if you get sick.'

'Did you dream I was going to get sick?' asked Lucy, despondently. 'Because last night I dreamed that we were separated. It's put me into a bad temper. I'm sorry.'

'I couldn't sleep last night at all,' he said.

'It was extremely confused,' she said, not bothering to move away from one of the dogs which was shaking itself down beside her. 'Water was everywhere of course, and we were crouched over our cans of food. The lightning was so bright I could see you, the dogs, in x-ray. One of the dogs had a bleeding muzzle.

'It rained without stopping. The dogs were whimpering at the sound of loud thunder. But we could only tell they were making noise from the inclination of their heads, the expression in their eyes. The only way any of us could communicate was through the outline of our mouths, our gestures. Thus we were all made equal, more equal than ever before, and we began our four-way conversation. The dog explained his bleeding muzzle. He said it was like his mouth watering when he saw food, except that his muzzle was bleeding at the prospect of death. Unfortunately, because he was a spotted sort of dog and inferior to the other, he couldn't control his bodily functions.

'He invited me to look into his eyes, saying and not saying: "You can read your future in the eyes of somebody else. My retina is like the silver on the back of a mirror." So I peered into his spaniel circles, realising, with some degree of horror, that my future was indeed myself. That the image so confining was me. That the only variation to be expected was that my right breast was slightly smaller than the left, that the down on my arm was brushed to the opposite side to which the mirror indicated.

'When I turned round you were gone, and the dog was licking its muzzle. I did not see you again until your corpse showed grey-brown on the surface of the fast-flowing creek.

'There was little choice for me now. I held the dog close by until the thunder began to fade, until it left with the voice of a tired char lady who'd just collected her pittance.'

'We must get you back to town,' he said, worried that she was developing a fever.

'We were all responsible for your death,' said Lucy. 'I'm so frightened. I don't think we should go back.'

'But your dream was a premonition of flood,' said Titus. 'Surely we're better off in town than out here.'

'I know you feel as frightened as I do,' said Lucy.

'No,' he lied, for the first time setting a barrier between them, on her behalf.

'We probably won't be able to get back anyway,' said Lucy, looking at the old model utility with its back wheels half in water.

'We can try. I've got spray to dry out the engine.'

'Why don't we wait a few days,' she said. Her determination surprised him. He took this as further evidence of her unhappiness, her desire to be back, warm and safe with her people.

'There is no choice.'

'But the rain's getting lighter,' said Lucy. 'The very lowest layer of cloud seems to be parting a little. See how it's parting.'

'I'll start packing,' he said.

As Titus placed each dripping item into the back of the

utility, Lucy watched with the grief of a mother whose children were leaving home. It seemed, at that moment, every element in her life was being loaded into that open truck. She could hear the distant playground voices of children grown up, of the priest at mass. How little it all added up to. Yet how important memories were to her; even more so in their doused-down tumble of disarray.

'Can I beg you,' said Lucy, in her most final voice, 'not to go back.'

'No,' said Titus, who had grown stubborn. He was sure she was frightened of her own weakness, of a desire to return to her people on compromising terms. 'What's the harm in going back? I think we should,' he said more softly.

He had forgotten his previous misgivings, and when all was loaded a squeal of wheel took them over slippery clay, through a wide arc of water, towards the Hermannsburg Road.

Lucy's hair was wet, like she remembered her father's had been, before he went out. Brylcreem, to look so *debonair*, she whispered to herself. Perhaps he had wet his hair as a warning of impermanence to his family. He'd had a rather rangy, dripping impermanence about his person. Under the light in the sitting room he'd seemed to glisten.

Her memories formed a womb of grey condensation in the car. She never imagined her father on dry turf, following the form in clean spats and panama hat. He'd always preferred the track in heavy weather, the camaraderie of the course on a wet day, closer to the night meetings that brought dog out of the grey and into the footlights.

'As soon as we get back into town,' said Titus, 'I'll have to check the level of the Todd.'

He looked into Lucy's eyes, remembering how at first they had seemed two salty blue mirages.

'But Matthew has a four-wheel drive that'll be able to get across.'

'Not necessarily,' said Titus, softly, attempting to part the damp strands of her hair.

'Hold on to the wheel,' laughed Lucy. 'We're skidding.'

'We're skidding whatever I do,' he said. 'Matthew will need supplies. The people who were camped in the bed of the Todd will be cold and looking for food. They'll go to him, and mother.'

'But Esther'll be prepared,' said Lucy.

'Up to a point. She doesn't like to plan too much. That's where I'm most different from her. She only plans when a situation is urgent, when she knows her plans will probably be too late anyway. So people will go to her hoping, not expecting.'

Why are you different?' asked Lucy, her curiosity deep as the intraversable puddles swirling with spent measuring sticks.

'I'm younger than she is,' he said. 'When you're young, you make plans. But one seems to grow out of them.'

'Like choice,' said Lucy, 'freely will, call it what you will, freely. It's a pattern. God given. At the beginning of the world there was choice, when the world was young Lucifer and Adam. At the end there will be no choice.

'Or if you prefer, in the beginning there was the illusion of choice, and at the end there will be the illusion of no choice. We can deal better in illusions.'

They arrived into town, tired and dispirited. Neither of them had really wanted to return. But they were back at the gloomy cave entrance of eucalypts and service stations. And they were soon down the empty corridor of the main street to reach the proud and spurting river.

There was only a fine mist of rain left. The town was closed, except for a number of souvenir shops selling spoons, tea towels, aboriginal women with man-high tits painted on black vaginal velvet.

They left their car to walk down to the river. There was a watchfulness about each vacant shop window, from where Lucy expected reluctant animals to emerge after the deluge, blinking their underground eyes.

As they passed the Anglican church, they could see a funeral was about to begin. People crowded into the vestibule, contracting the bat ribs of their umbrellas. Still outside was a group of men, waiting to finish their cigarettes. When they saw Titus and Lucy, arm in arm, they became angry, pushing through the mist to obtain a confrontation.

'What are you doing here?' asked one of them. His name was Daley. Mr Harrison had once brought him to class.

'We're going down to the river,' said Titus.

'Don't bother, mate,' said one of the men. 'The evidence's been washed away.'

Being in a group gave these men authority. They bunched obstructively.

'Is it Sandy Morton's funeral?' asked Titus, expecting confirmation.

'I don't believe it,' said Daley, addressing the group with savage finesse. 'You don't have to put on an act. We're not the police.'

'I've been out bush,' said Titus, 'with Lucy.' He watched the muscles on their necks expand with hate.

'Then get back out of town,' said the smallest of them, 'and keep fucking Lucy. Sandy Morton's dead.'

'The rapist at the funeral. How appropriate,' said Daley. 'If I had my way I'd wring your bloody neck.'

His statement opened up a range of possibilities to the others. The grey sky was adding an extra dimension to these men who, in the dry blue intensity of past weather, had looked like cardboard cutouts with sharp childish edges.

They decided they would take Titus now, as they had

done years ago, in similar cases. They pushed in on him. He was taller. They looked awkward as they held him, like runty escorts at a dance. Their arms bulged, out of proportion to the restraint needed.

Lucy, unable to speak, concentrated her efforts on movement. She would have to get Father Scarf. Esther and Matthew were on the other side of the river.

When Titus saw her running away from him, disappointment caused him to stop struggling. His body became heavy and resigned to the trundling motions which pushed him further and further down the street.

'Thank God,' said Lucy, as she saw the priest working in the presbytery garden. 'Come quickly. Some men have got Titus. They're taking him in the direction of the Todd.'

'In a car?'

'No.'

'We'll catch them then,' he said. 'What's happened?'

'They said he killed Sandy Morton.'

The two ran quickly to the river, calling for help from the passers by. There was no response. The eyes of these people were glassy and dead as they walked steadily in the direction of the river.

'I'll get the police,' said Vivian. 'That's all we can do.'

At the station, lone Constable MacPhee said that as soon as he'd spelled the name he'd send someone down in due course.

By the time Father Scarf arrived at the river, a crowd had gathered. It seemed poised on the edge of the river bank, as if the very novelty of seeing water was a call to jump.

Titus was hanging from a gum tree, leaning partly across the swift water. One of the men had collected strong rope from the back of his truck.

Lucy struggled to reach her lover. His dear face was distorted, his legs jerking against the body's weight. Two of the men held her back. Father Scarf was also being held.

Lucy jerked her body violently in unison with Titus. But he couldn't see her. The rain had begun to fall heavily again, adding weight to his convulsions.

The tree branch broke.

Titus fell to the ground. Saved by the wetness, the softness, of the big eucalypt.

The people around him were shocked by such miraculous complicity. The rain fell heavily in rope. Disorganised, they allowed him to escape.

Titus fled along the perimeter of the river, with the gracelessness of one betrayed.

Lucy watched, barely able to glimpse his movements. How well the country worked for him.

Heavy with loss, she looked into the empty eyes of her captors, realising, even as their grips loosened, that the sweet, the brief time of freedom had passed.